CAMBRIDGE LIBRARY COLLECTION

Books of enduring scholarly value

English Men of Letters

In the 1870s, Macmillan publishers began to issue a series of books called 'English Men of Letters' – biographies of English writers by other English writers. The general editor of the series was the journalist, critic, politician, and supporter (and later biographer) of Gladstone, John Morley (1838–1923). The aim was to provide a short introduction to each subject and his works, but also that the life should illuminate the works, and vice versa. The subjects range chronologically from Chaucer to Thackeray and Dickens, and an important feature of the series is that many of the authors (Henry James on Hawthorne, Ward on Dickens) were discussing writers of the previous generation, and some (Trollope on Thackeray) had even known their subjects personally. The series exemplifies the British approach to literary biography and criticism at the end of the nineteenth century, and also reveals which authors were at that time regarded as canonical.

Macaulay

Historian, essayist and poet, Thomas Babington Macaulay (1800–59) is described by his biographer as possessing a mind that was born wise and nurtured to a state of brilliance. With an ability to imbue his most scholarly works with a narrative power 'on a level with that of the greatest masters of prose fiction', Macaulay's multi-volume *History of England* assured his fame in middle-class Victorian households. Nevertheless, few today are familiar with the author's personal history. Published in the first series of English Men of Letters in 1882, this biography by James Cotter Morison (1832–88) introduces readers to the main influences on Macaulay's life and work from his childhood, through his days at Trinity College, Cambridge, to the writing of his *History*. The result is a sympathetic and detailed portrait of a man whose life was shaped by literature.

T0382633

Cambridge University Press has long been a pioneer in the reissuing of out-of-print titles from its own backlist, producing digital reprints of books that are still sought after by scholars and students but could not be reprinted economically using traditional technology. The Cambridge Library Collection extends this activity to a wider range of books which are still of importance to researchers and professionals, either for the source material they contain, or as landmarks in the history of their academic discipline.

Drawing from the world-renowned collections in the Cambridge University Library, and guided by the advice of experts in each subject area, Cambridge University Press is using state-of-the-art scanning machines in its own Printing House to capture the content of each book selected for inclusion. The files are processed to give a consistently clear, crisp image, and the books finished to the high quality standard for which the Press is recognised around the world. The latest print-on-demand technology ensures that the books will remain available indefinitely, and that orders for single or multiple copies can quickly be supplied.

The Cambridge Library Collection will bring back to life books of enduring scholarly value (including out-of-copyright works originally issued by other publishers) across a wide range of disciplines in the humanities and social sciences and in science and technology.

Macaulay

J. COTTER MORISON

CAMBRIDGE
UNIVERSITY PRESS

CAMBRIDGE UNIVERSITY PRESS

Cambridge, New York, Melbourne, Madrid, Cape Town,
Singapore, São Paolo, Delhi, Tokyo, Mexico City

Published in the United States of America by Cambridge University Press, New York

www.cambridge.org
Information on this title: www.cambridge.org/9781108034531

© in this compilation Cambridge University Press 2011

This edition first published 1882
This digitally printed version 2011

ISBN 978-1-108-03453-1 Paperback

English Men of Letters

EDITED BY JOHN MORLEY

MACAULAY

MACAULAY

BY

J. COTTER MORISON

London:

MACMILLAN AND CO.

1882.

CONTENTS.

MACAULAY

MACAULAY.

CHAPTER I.

(A.D. 1800—1841.)

THE prosperity which attended Macaulay all through life
may be said to have begun with the moment of his birth.
Of all good gifts which it is in the power of fortune to
bestow, none can surpass the being born of wise, honourable, and tender parents : and this lot fell to him. He
came of a good stock, though not of the kind most recog-
nized by Colleges of Arms. Descended from Scotch
Presbyterians—ministers many of them—on his father's
side, and from a Quaker family on his mother's, he probably united as many guarantees of "good birth" in the
moral sense of the words, as could be found in these islands
at the beginning of the century. His mother (*née* Selina
Mills) appears to have been a woman of warm-hearted
and affectionate temper, yet clear-headed and firm withal,
and with a good eye for the influences which go to the
formation of character. Though full of a young mother's
natural pride at the talent and mental precocity of her
eldest son, the subject of this volume, Thomas Babing-

B

ton Macaulay (born October 25, 1800), she was wise
enough to eschew even the semblance of spoiling. The
boy found, like many studious children, that he could
spend his time with more pleasure, and probably with more
profit, in reading at home than in lessons at school, and
consequently exerted daily that passive resistance against
leaving home which many mothers have not the strength
to overcome. Mrs. Macaulay always met appeals grounded
on the unfavourableness of the weather, with the stoical
answer : " No, Tom ; if it rains cats and dogs you shall go."
As a mere infant, his knowledge, and his power of working it up into literary form, were equally extraordinary.
Compositions in prose and verse, histories, epics, odes, and
hymns flowed with equal freedom, and correctness in
point of language, from his facile pen. He was regarded,
as he well deserved to be, as a prodigy, not only by his
parents, but by others who might be presumed to be less
partial critics. Mrs. Hannah More, who in certain circles
almost assumed the character of a female Dr. Johnson, and
director of taste, pronounced little Macaulay's hymns
" quite extraordinary for such a baby." The wise mother
treasured these things in her heart, but carefully shielded
her child from the corrupting influences of early flattery.
" You will believe," she writes, " that we never appear
to regard anything he does as anything more than a
schoolboy's amusement." Genuine maternal tenderness,
without a trace of weak indulgence, seems to have
marked this excellent woman's treatment of her children.
When once he fell ill at school, she came and nursed
him with such affection that years afterwards he referred
to the circumstance with vivid emotion :—

There is nothing I remember with so much pleasure as the
time when you nursed me at Aspenden. How sick and sleepless

and weak I was, lying in bed, when I was told that you were come. How well I remember with what an ecstasy of joy I saw that face approaching me. The sound of your voice, the touch of your hand, are present to me now, and will be, I trust in God, to my last hour.

But many a devoted mother could watch by the sick-bed of her son for weeks without sleep, who would not have the courage to keep him up to a high standard of literary performance. When he was not yet thirteen she wrote to him :—

I know you write with great ease to yourself, and would rather write ten poems than prune one. All your pieces are much mended after a little reflection ; therefore, take your solitary walks and think over each separate thing. Spare no time or trouble, and render each piece as perfect as you can, and then leave the event without one anxious thought. I have always admired a saying of one of the old heathen philosophers ; when a friend was condoling with him that he so well deserved of the gods, and yet they did not shower their favours on him as on some others less worthy, he answered, " I will continue to deserve well of them." So do you, my dearest.

Deep, sober, clear-eyed love watched over Macaulay's childhood. His mother lived long enough to see her son on the high road to honour and fame, and died almost immediately after he had made his first great speech on the Reform Bill in 1831.

His father, Zachary, was a man cast in an heroic mould, who reproduced, one might surmise, the moral features of some stern old Scotch Covenanter among his ancestors, and never quite fitted into the age in which it was his lot to live. There was a latent faculty in him which, in spite of his long and laborious life, he was never able completely to unfold. A silent, austere, earnest, patient, enduring man, almost wholly without the gift of speech, and the power of uttering the deep, involved thought that was in him— a man after Carlyle's own heart, if he could have seen anything good in an emancipator of negroes. A feeling of respect bordering on reverence is excited by the little we know of Macaulay's father—his piety, his zeal, his self-sacrifice to the cause to which he devoted his mind, body, and estate; even the gloom and moroseness of his latter years, all point to a character of finer fibre and loftier strain, many might be disposed to think, than that of his eloquent and brilliant son. There are parallel cases on record of men endowed with over-abundance of thought and feeling, for which they never find adequate expression, who have had sons in whose case the spell which sealed their own lips to silence is broken—sons who can find ready utterance for the burden of thought which lay imprisoned in their sires, partly because they were not *overfull*, as their fathers were. Diderot was such a case. He always said that he was not to be compared to his father, the cutler of Langres; and declared he was never so pleased in his life as when a fellow-townsman said to him, " Ah, M. Diderot, you are a very famous man, but you will never be half the man your father was." Carlyle always spoke of his father in similar language. But the closest analogy to the two Macaulays is that of the two Mirabeaus, the crabbed, old " friend of man," and the erratic genius, the orator Gabrielle Honoré. It is certainly "a likeness in unlikeness" of no common kind; and nothing can be more dissimilar than the two pairs of men; but the similarity of relation of elder to younger in the two cases is all the more remarkable.

In this grave, well-ordered home Macaulay passed a happy childhood. He had three brothers and five sisters,

all his juniors, and for them he always felt a fraternal
affection which bordered on a passion. His trials, as
already implied, commenced when he had to leave his
books, his parents, and his playmates for a distant school
in the neighbourhood of Cambridge. Time never seems
to have completely assuaged his home-sickness; and his
letters to his mother express in a style of precocious
maturity, the artless yearnings and affectionate grief of a
child. Nothing more dutiful, tender, and intelligent, can
well be conceived. His second half-year seems to have
been even more painful to bear than the first; his biographer, will not print the letter he wrote immediately after
his return to school at the end of the summer holidays—
it would be " too cruel." This is the second—written two
months before he had ended his thirteenth year :—

Shelford, August 14, 1813.

MY DEAR MAMA,—I must confess that I have been a little
disappointed at not receiving a letter from home to-day. I hope,
however, for one to-morrow. My spirits are far more depressed
by leaving home than they were last half-year. Everything
brings home to my recollection. Everything I read, or see, or
hear brings it to my mind. You told me I should be happy
when I once came here, but not an hour passes in which I do not
shed tears at thinking of home. Every hope, however unlikely
to be realized, affords me some small consolation. The
morning on which I went, you told me that possibly I might
come home before the holidays. If you can confirm that hope,
believe me when I assure you there is nothing which I would
not give for one instant's sight of home. Tell me in your next,
expressly, if you can, whether or no there is any likelihood of my
coming home before the holidays. If I could gain Papa's leave,
I should select my birthday, October 25, as the time which I
should wish to spend at that home which absence renders still
dearer to me. I think I see you sitting by Papa just after his

dinner, reading my letter, and turning to him with an inquisitive glance at the end of the paragraph. I think, too, that I see his expressive shake of the head at it. O, may I be mistaken! You cannot conceive what an alteration a favourable answer would produce on me. If your approbation of my request depends upon my advancing in study, I will work like a cart-horse. If you should refuse it, you will deprive me of the most pleasing illusion which I ever experienced in my life. Pray do not fail to write speedily.—Your dutiful and affectionate son,

T. B. MACAULAY

The urgent and pathetic appeal was not successful. The stern father did shake his head as the boy had feared, and the " pleasing illusion " was not realized.

His school, though a private one, was of a superior kind. There he laid the foundation of his future scholarship. But what surprises most, is that in the midst of the usually engrossing occupation of a diligent schoolboy, with his Latin, Greek, and mathematics, he found time to gratify that insatiable thirst for European literature which he retained through life. Before he was fifteen we find him recommending his mother to read Boccacio, at least in Dryden's metrical version, and weighing him against Chaucer, to whom he "infinitely prefers him." This shows, at any rate, that no Puritanic surveillance directed his choice of books. The fault seems to have been rather the other way, and he enjoyed an excess of liberty, in being allowed to indulge almost without restraint his strong partiality for the lighter and more attractive forms of literature, to the neglect of austerer studies. Poetry and prose fiction remained through life Macaulay's favourite reading. And there is no evidence that he at any time was ever submitted by his teachers or himself, to a mental discipline of a more bracing kind. His father apparently considered that the formation of his son's mind, was no part of his duty. Engrossed in his crusade against slavery, in which cause " he laboured as men labour for the honours of a profession, or for the subsistence of their children," he left the mental training of young Macaulay to hired teachers—except in one particular, which will be readily divined. The principles of evangelical religion were inculcated with more zeal and persistence than discretion. It is the ever-recurring error of old and serious minds, to think that the loftier views of life and duty, the moral beliefs which they themselves, in the course of years, after a long experience, perhaps of a very different code of ethics, have acquired, can be transplanted by precept, full-grown and vigorous, into the minds of the young. The man of fifty, forgetting his own youth, or remembering it only with horror, wishes his son to think and feel and act as he does himself. He should wish him the languid pulse and failing vigour of decay at the same time. In any case, the attempt to impart " vital religion " to Macaulay signally failed, and possibly was the indirect cause of the markedly unspiritual tone of his writings, and of his resolute silence on questions of ultimate beliefs. The son's taste for poetry, novels, and " worldly literature " produced a suspicious querulousness in the elder Macaulay, which cannot easily be excused. He listened with a too indulgent ear to vague complaints against his son's carriage and conversation, demanding answers to the anonymous accusations, in a tone little calculated to inspire sympathy. It says very much for Macaulay's sweetness of character, that he was never soured or estranged from his father by this injudicious treatment. On the contrary, he remained a loyal and dutiful son, under trials, as we shall see, of no common severity.

In October, 1818, he went as a commoner to Trinity College, Cambridge. Neither his taste nor his acquirements were fitted to win him distinction in the special studies of the place. In his boyhood he had shown a transient liking for mathematics; but this had given way to an intense repugnance for exact science. "I can scarcely bear," he says in a letter to his mother, "to write on mathematics, or mathematicians. Oh! for words to express my abomination of that science, if a name sacred to the useful and embellishing arts may be applied to the perception and recollection of certain properties in numbers and figures. Oh! that I had to learn astrology, demonology, or school divinity. . . . . Oh to change Cam for Isis." His inclination was wholly for literature. Unfortunately according to the regulations then in force a minimum of honours in mathematics was an indispensable condition for competing for the Chancellor's medals—the test of classical proficiency before the institution of the classical tripos. Macaulay failed even to obtain the lowest place among the Junior Optimes, and was, what is called in University parlance, gulphed. But he won the prize for Latin declamation, he twice gained the Chancellor's medals for English verse, and by winning a Craven scholarship he sufficiently proved his classical attainments. Why he was not sent to Oxford, as it seems he would have preferred, does not appear. Probably religious scruples on his father's part had something to do with the choice of a University. Otherwise, Oxford would have appeared to offer obvious advantages to a young man with his bent. His disproportionate partiality for the lighter sides of literature met with no corrective at Cambridge. As he could not assimilate the mathematical training, he practically got very little. The poets, orators, and historians,

read with a view chiefly to their language, formed a very
imperfect discipline for a mind in which fancy and imagination rather needed the curb than the spur. A course
of what at Oxford is technically called "science," even as
then understood, would have been an invaluable gymnastic
for Macaulay, and would have strengthened faculties in
his mind, which as a matter of fact never received adequate
culture. We shall have repeated occasion in subsequent
chapters to notice his want of philosophic grasp, his dread·
and dislike of arduous speculation, his deficient courage
in facing intellectual problems. It is not probable that
any education would have made him a deep and vigorous
thinker; but we can hardly doubt that a more austere
training would at least have preserved him from some of
the errors into which he habitually fell.

As it was, not Cambridge studies but Cambridge society
left a mark on his mind. Genial and frank, and with an
unlimited passion and talent for talk, he made troops of
friends, and before he left the University had acquired a
reputation as one of the best conversationists of the day.
He met his equals in the Coleridges, Hyde and Charles
Villiers, Romilly, Praed, and in one case his superior in
verbal dialectics, Charles Austin, of whom Mill in one
sentence has drawn such a powerful sketch: "The impression which he gave was that of boundless strength,
together with talents which, combined with such apparent
force of will and character, seemed capable of dominating
the world." Of their wit combats a story is told, which
slightly savours of mythus, how at Bowood the two Can-
tabs got engaged in a discussion at breakfast, and such
was the splendour and copiousness of their talk, that the
whole company in the house, "ladies, artists, politicians,
diners-out," listened entranced till it was time to dress for

dinner. It is needless to say that Macaulay shone among
the brightest in the Union Debating Society. Thus those
faculties which were naturally strong were made stronger,
those which were naturally weak received little or no
exercise.

After literature, Macaulay's strongest taste was for politics. His father's house at Clapham was a common meet-
ing-ground for politicians engaged in the agitation against
slavery ; and when yet a boy he had learned to take an
interest in public affairs. In the free atmosphere of
undergraduate discussion, such an interest is the last
which is allowed to lie dormant, and Macaulay soon
became a strenuous politician. Then occurred his single
change of opinions throughout life. He went up to Cambridge a Tory; Charles Austin soon made him a Whig, or
something more ; and before his first year of residence at
Cambridge was over, he had to defend himself against the
exaggerated reports of some talebearer who had alarmed
his parents. He protests that he is not a "son of anarchy
and confusion," as his mother had been led to believe. The
particular charge seems to have been that he had been
" initiated into democratical societies " in the University,
and that he had spoken of the so-called Manchester massacre in terms of strong indignation. It would have said
little for his generosity and public spirit if he had not.

It is not easy for us now to realize the condition of
England in Macaulay's youth. Though so little remote
in point of time, and though still remembered by old men
who are yet among us, the state of public affairs between
the peace of 1815 and the passing of the Reform Bill was
so unlike anything to which we are accustomed, that a
certain effort is required to make it present to the mind.
It is not easy to conceive a state of things in which the

country was covered by an army of "common informers," whose business it was to denounce the non-payment of taxes, and share with the fisc the onerous fines imposed, often without a shadow of justice,—in which marauders roamed at night under the command of "General Ludd," and terrorized whole counties,—when the Habeas Corpus Act was suspended, and "in Suffolk, nightly, fires of incendiaries began to blaze in every district,"—when mobs of labourers assembled with flags bearing the motto "Bread or Blood," and riots occurred in London, Nottingham, Leicester, and Derby, culminating in the massacre at Manchester,—when at last the famous Six Acts were passed, which surrendered the liberties of Englishmen into the hands of the Government. "The old spirit of liberty would appear to have departed from England, when public meetings could not be held without the licence of magistrates, when private houses might be searched for arms, when a person convicted a second time of publishing a libel "[1]—that is, a criticism on the Government—"might be transported beyond the seas." Macaulay had been a year at College when the Six Acts were passed. (Dec. 1819.)

Nothing could be more characteristic than the way in which Macaulay kept his head in this semi-revolutionary condition of public affairs. A man of strong passions would, inevitably, have taken an extreme side—either for reaction, or reform. Civil society seemed threatened by the anarchists; civil liberty seemed equally threatened by the Government. Either extreme Tory or extreme Radical opinions would appear to have been the only choice for an ardent young spirit—and the latter the more suitable to the impetuosity of youth and genius. Macaulay

[1] Knight's *History of England*, vol. viii. cap. 4.

took his stand, with the premature prudence and wisdom
of a veteran, on the judicious compromise of sound Whig
principles.   He was zealous for reform, but never was
touched by a breath of revolutionary fervour.   The
grinding collision of Old and New principles of Government did not set him on fire either with fear or with
hope.   The menacing invasions on the old system of
Church and State, which had wrecked the happiness of
the last years of Burke—which now disturbed the rest
of such men as Southey, Coleridge, Wordsworth—filled
him with no dismay.   But he was as little caught up
by visions of a new dawn—of a future " all the brighter
that the past was base."   In the heyday of youth and
spirits and talent, he took his side with the old and
practical Whigs, who were well on their guard against
" too much zeal," but who saw their way to such reforms
as could be realized in the conditions of the time.
He was a Whig by necessity of nature, by calmness of
passion, combined with superlative common sense.

He did not get a Fellowship till his third and last trial,
in 1824.   He had then already begun to make a name in
literature.   As a Junior Bachelor he competed for the
Greaves historical prize—" On the Conduct and Character
of William the Third."   The essay is still in existence,
though only the briefest fragments of it have been published, which are interesting on more grounds than one.
Not only is the subject the same as that which occupied
so many years of his later life, but the style is already
his famous style in all essential features.   There is no
mistaking this : —

Lewis XIV. was not a great general.   He was not a great
legislator.   But he was in one sense of the word a great King.
He was perfect master of all the mysteries of the science of

royalty—of the arts which at once extend power and conciliate popularity, which most advantageously display the merits and most dexterously conceal the deficiencies of a sovereign.

This essay shows that his style was quite natural, and unaffected. Whatever may be thought of Macaulay's style by the present race of critics, no one will deny that it was original, and has left a mark on our literature, like all original styles which give an impression of novelty on their first appearance : it was, we see, his spontaneous mode of utterance. The true prose writer, equally with the true poet, is born, not made.

More important were his contributions to Knight's *Quarterly Magazine.* Spirited verse, prose, fiction, and criticism on poets, were his first efforts in literature, and prove sufficiently, if proof were wanted, in what direction his calling lay. Two battle-pieces in metre, *Ivry* and *Naseby,* still live by reason of their vigour and animation, and are little, if at all, inferior to his later productions in verse. The *Fragments of a Roman Tale,* and the *Scenes from the Athenian Revels,* are so sparkling and vivacious, and show such a natural turn for a dialogue and dramatic *mise en scène,* that it says a great deal for Macaulay's good sense and literary conscientiousness that he remained content with this first success, and did not continue to work a vein which would have brought him prompt, if ephemeral, popularity. There can be little doubt that he could have equalled, or surpassed, most historical novelists who have written since Scott. But he had too genuine a love of history not to be conscious of the essential hollowness and unreality of the historical novel, and he never meddled with it again. Of the two criticisms on Dante and Petrarch, the first is nearly as

good as anything Macaulay ever wrote in that style
(which, to be sure, is not saying much, as he was almost
incapable of analyzing and exhibiting the beauties in the
great creative works which he admired so much) ; but its
generous enthusiasm and zeal for the great Florentine,
and indeed, for Italian literature generally, are really
touching, and produce an effect on the mind not usually
produced by his criticisms.

But by far the most noteworthy of his contributions
to Knight's *Magazine* was the *Conversation between Mr
Abraham Cowley and Mr. John Milton, touching the great
Civil War.* We are told that it was his own decided
favourite among his earlier efforts in literature ; and most
correct was his judgment. The introduction to the
dialogue, for simplicity and grace is worthy of Plato :—

" It chanced in the warm and beautiful spring of the year 1665,
a little before the saddest summer that ever London saw," begins
the narrator, " that I went to the Bowling Green at Piccadilly,
whither at that time the best gentry made continual resort.
There I met Mr. Cowley, who had lately left Barmelms. . . . .
I entreated him to dine with me at my lodging in the Temple,
which he most courteously promised. And that so eminent a
guest might not lack better entertainment than cooks or vintners
can provide, I sent to the house of Mr. John Milton, in the
Artillery Walk, to beg that he would also be my guest, for I
hoped that they would think themselves rather united by their
common art than divided by their different factions. And so,
indeed, it proved. For while we sat at table they talked freely
of men and things, as well ancient as modern, with much civility.
Nay, Mr. Milton, who seldom tasted wine, both because of his
singular temperance and because of his gout, did more than
once pledge Mr. Cowley, who was indeed no hermit in diet.
At last, being heated, Mr. Milton begged that I would open the
windows. ' Nay,' said I, ' if you desire fresh air and coolness,

what would hinder us, as the evening is fair, from sailing for an hour on the river ? ' To this they both cheerfully consented ; and forth we walked, Mr. Cowley and I leading Mr. Milton between us to the Temple Stairs. There we took a boat, and thence we were rowed up the river.

" The wind was pleasant, the evening fine ; the sky, the earth, and the water beautiful to look upon. But Mr. Cowley and I held our peace, and said nothing of the gay sights around us, lest we should too feelingly remind Mr. Milton of his calamity, whereof he needed no monitor ; for soon he said sadly : ' Ah, Mr. Cowley, you are a happy man. What would I now give but for one more look at the sun, and the waters, and the gardens of this fair city ! ' "

There is reason to think that Macaulay's splendid literary faculty was seriously damaged by his early entrance into the conflict of party politics, and that he never wholly recovered from its effect. It destroyed the tender bloom of his mind. As Mr. Pattison has shown that even Milton, when he turned from *Comus* and *Lycidas* to write ferocious pamphlets for twenty years, " left behind him the golden age, and one half of his poetic genius," [2] so may we say of Macaulay, that when he turned from such work as this dialogue to parliamentary debate and the distractions of office, he did an injury to his prose, which is none the less great and deplorable because it cannot be accurately measured. But let any one read this beautiful piece of majestic English, then any passage of the History or the Essays which he may like best, and say whether letters have not lost far more than politics have gained by Macaulay's entrance into Parliament. The conduct of the whole dialogue is masterly. Both Milton and Cowley

[2] *Milton*, by Mark Pattison, in this series.

sustain their parts with admirable propriety. It is no
sham fight in which one of the interlocutors is a man of
straw, set up only to be knocked down. The most
telling arguments on the Royalists' side are put into
Cowley's mouth, and enunciated with a force which cannot
be surpassed. Above all, the splendour and nobility of
the diction are such as never visited Macaulay's vigils
again. The piece is hardly ever referred to, and appears
to be forgotten. Even his most loyal biographer and
kinsman waxes cold and doubtful about it. But it
remains, and will be remembered, as a promise and pledge
of literary power which adverse fate hindered him from
fully redeeming.

Macaulay's early success in literature did not improve
his relations with his father. On the contrary, he appears
to have been chidden for everything he wrote. The
ground of complaint was not far to seek : the Magazine in
which he wrote was a worldly periodical, in which the
interests of religion were neglected or offended. The
sympathies of most readers will be so strongly in favour
of the son, that we cannot do wrong in casting a look of
forlorn commiseration on the old Puritan, who felt, with
an anguish perhaps never fully expressed, the conviction
and the proof growing on him that his son's heart was
not as his heart, and that they were parting company
as regards the deepest subjects more and more. When
Macaulay was a lad at school his father had written to
him : "I do long and pray most earnestly that the ornament of a meek and quiet spirit may be substituted for
vehemence and self-confidence." The good man's hopes
and prayers had not been realized, nor was his treatment
of his son such that their realization could be expected.
But the sense of void and inner bereavement would be

none the less bitter and strange even if the faults of treatment were perceived when it was too late to rectify them, and of this feeling on the father's part there is no evidence. In any case, on no occasion in life did Macaulay show the generosity and tenderness of his nature more admirably than in these seasons of trial and failing sympathy with his father.   Troubles without were added to troubles within.   When he went to Cambridge his father seemed in prosperous fortune which bordered on affluence.   It was understood that he was to be "made in a modest way an eldest son."   But a great change had come over Zachary Macaulay's neglected business.   The firm wanted a competent head.   The elder partner gave his mind, his time, and his energy to the agitation against the slave-trade. The junior partner, Babington, was not a man to supply his place.   Like Cobden many years afterwards, the elder Macaulay neglected his private affairs for public interests, and he quietly slid down the road which leads to commercial ruin.   Then the son showed the sterling stuff of which he was made.   He received the first ill-news at Cambridge with "a frolick welcome" of courage and filial devotion.   "He was firmly prepared," he said, "to encounter the worst with fortitude, and to do his utmost to retrieve it by exertion."   A promise kept to the letter and to the spirit.   Not only did he, with the help of his brother Henry, pay off ultimately his father's debts, but he became a second father to his brothers and sisters.

He quietly took up the burden which his father was unable to bear; and before many years had elapsed the fortunes of all for whose welfare he considered himself responsible were abundantly secured.   In the course of the efforts which he expended on the accomplishment of this result, he unlearned the

c

very notion of framing his method of life with a view to his own
pleasure; and such was his high and simple nature that it may
well be doubted whether it ever crossed his mind that to live
wholly for others was a sacrifice at all.[3]

This was much, and inexpressibly noble; but even this
was not all. Not only did Macaulay not give a thought
to his own frustrated hopes and prospects; not only did
he, a young man, shoulder the burden of a family two
generations deep, but he did it with the sunniest radiance,
as if not a care rankled in his heart. His sister, Lady
Trevelyan, says that those who did not know him then
" never knew him in his most brilliant, witty, and fertile
vein." He was life and sunshine to young and old in the
sombre house in Great Ormond Street, where the forlorn
old father like a blighted oak lingered on in leafless decay,
reading one long sermon to his family on Sunday afternoons,
and another long sermon on Sunday evenings—" where
Sunday walking for walking's sake was never allowed, and
even going to a distant church was discouraged." Through
this Puritanic gloom Macaulay shot like a sunbeam, and
turned it into a fairy scene of innocent laughter and
mirth. Against Macaulay the author severe things, and as
just as severe, may be said; but as to his conduct
in his own home—as a son, as a brother, and an uncle
—it is only the barest justice to say that he appears to
have touched the furthest verge of human virtue, sweetness, and generosity. His thinking was often, if not
generally, pitched in what we must call a low key, but his
action might put the very saints to shame. He reversed
a practice too common among men of genius, who are often
careful to display all their shining and attractive qualities

[3] *Trevelyan*, vol. i. cap. 3.

to the outside world, and keep for home consumption their meanness, selfishness, and ill-temper. Macaulay struck no heroic attitude of benevolence, magnanimity, and aspiration before the world—rather the opposite; but in the circle of his home affections he practised those virtues without letting his right hand know what was done by his left.

He was called to the bar in 1826, and went more than once on the Northern Circuit. But he did not take kindly to the law, got little or no practice, and soon renounced all serious thoughts of the legal profession, even if he ever entertained any. He had, indeed, in the mean time found something a great deal better to do. In October, 1824, writing to his father, he said, "When I see you in London I will mention to you a piece of secret history," which he conceals for the moment, This referred to an invitation to write for the *Edinburgh Review ;* and in the following August, 1825, appeared an article on Milton, which at once arrested the attention of the public, and convinced the shrewder judges that a new force had arisen in literature. The success was splendid and decisive, and produced a great peal of fame. He followed it up with rapid energy, and with his single hand gave a new life to the *Edinburgh Review.* He was already distinguished even in the select circle of promising young men. In 1828 Lord Lyndhurst made him a Commissioner of Bankruptcy. In 1830 his articles on Mill had so struck Lord Lansdowne that he offered him, though quite a stranger, a seat in Parliament for the borough of Calne.

He was now thirty years old. He was a finished classical scholar, and a master of English and Italian literature. French literature he no doubt knew well, but not with the same intimacy and sympathy. Of English history he already possessed the seventeenth and eighteenth centuries with rare accuracy and grasp. And of all history, ancient or modern, he probably had a competent command. On the other hand, his want of philosophical training does not appear to have been corrected by subsequent studies of a severer kind. All higher speculation seems to have been antipathetic to him. He spoke with respect of Bentham, but there is no evidence that he ever assimilated Bentham's doctrines. He admired Coleridge's poetry, but he did not meddle with his philosophy—which certainly was not very much, but still it was the best representative of speculative thought in England, and full of attraction to ardent young minds. In after-years, when Macaulay ventured to handle religious and philosophical subjects of a certain depth, this defect in his education made itself felt very plainly. But for the present, and for some time after, it was not perceived. He was abundantly well prepared by natural acuteness and wide reading to make more than a creditable figure amid the loose talk and looser thinking which are the ordinary staple of politics, and to politics he had now come in earnest.

Entering Parliament a few months before the death of George IV., he was just in time to witness the great battle of Reform fought out from beginning to end; to take, indeed, a conspicuous and honourable share in the campaign and final victory. His first speech on the Reform Bill placed him in the first rank of orators, if not of debaters. The Speaker sent for him, and " told him that in all his prolonged experience he had never seen the House in such a state of excitement." [4] Sir Robert Peel paid him a most handsome compliment ; and another member was heard to say that he had not heard such speaking since

[4] *Trevelyan*, vol. I., cap. 4.

Fox. There can, indeed, be no doubt about the impressiveness and weight of Macaulay's speaking.   " Whenever he
rose to speak," says Mr. Gladstone, who sat with him in
Parliament nearly from the first, " it was a summons like
a trumpet-call to fill the benches." It may well be questioned whether Macaulay was so well endowed for any
career as that of a great orator.   The rapidity of speech
suited the impetuosity of his genius far better than the
slow labour of composition. He has the true Demosthenic
rush in which argument becomes incandescent with
passion.   To read his speeches by themselves, isolated
from the debate in which they were delivered, is to do
them injustice.   It is only when we read them in *Han-
sard* or other contemporary reports, that we see how far
higher was their plane of thought than that of the best
speaking to which they were opposed, or even to that on
his own side.   It is not going too far to say that he
places the question on loftier grounds of state policy than
any of his colleagues.   In his fourth speech on the Reform
Bill, brushing away with disdain the minuter sophistries
and special pleading of his opponents, he tells them that
the Bill must be carried or the country will be ruined—
that it will be carried whatever they do, but carried by
revolution and civil war.   " You may make the change
tedious, you may make it violent, you may—God in his
mercy forbid—you may make it bloody, but avert it you
cannot."   Even if it were a bad bill, it should be passed, as
the less of two evils, compared to withholding it.   Then
he throws those harpoons of pointed epigram, which are
rarely at the command of orators who are not also writers,
and which are as wise and true as they are sharp :

What then, it is said, would you legislate in haste ?   Would you legislate in times of great excitement concerning matters of such deep concern ? Yes, sir, I would ; and if any bad consequences should follow from the haste and excitement, let those be answerable who, when there was no need of haste, when there existed no excitement, refused to listen to any project of reform ; nay, made it an argument against reform that the public mind was not excited. . . . . I allow that hasty legislation is an evil. *But reformers are compelled to legislate fast just because bigots will not legislate early.* Reformers are compelled to legislate in times of excitement, because bigots will not legislate in times of tranquillity.

Nothing shows more clearly the impression made by this magnificent speech than the pains taken by the Opposition to answer it. Croker, who rose immediately after Macaulay sat down, devoted a two hours' speech exclusively to answering him ; and Croker was one of the ablest debaters of his party. All the best men on that side followed the same line, feeling that Macaulay was really the formidable man. Sir Robert Inglis, Sir Charles Wetherell, Praed, and, finally, the Ajax of the Tories, Sir Robert Peel himself, singled out the "honourable and learned member" for Calne, as the foeman most worthy of their steel. No compliment could surpass this.

From the time he entered Parliament till nearly four years afterwards, when he sailed for India, Macaulay's life was one of strenuous and incessant labour, such as has been hardly ever surpassed in the lives of the busiest men. Besides his Parliamentary duties he had official work—first as Commissioner, and then as Secretary, to the Board of Control ; and in consequence of the frequent indisposition of his chief, Mr. Charles Grant, the whole labour of the office often devolved upon him. He was one of the lions of London Society, and a constant guest

at Holland House—the imperious mistress of which
scolded, flattered, and caressed him with a patronizing
condescension, that would not have been to every person's taste. He was on intimate terms with Rogers,
Moore, Campbell, Luttrel, and the other wits of the day,
and he more than held his own as a talker and a wit.
And all this time he was writing those articles for the
Edinburgh Review, which perhaps are often unwittingly
assumed to have been his main occupation. They were
in truth struck off in hastily snatched moments of leisure,
saved with a miserly thrift from public and official work,
by rising at five and writing till breakfast. Thirteen
articles, from the *Essay on Robert Montgomery* to the
first *Essay on Lord Chatham* inclusive, were written
amidst these adverse conditions. We are bound in common equity to remember this fact, when inclined to find
fault with either the matter or the manner of Macaulay's
Essays. They were not the meditated compositions of a
student wooing his muse in solitude and repose, crooning
over his style and maturing his thought ; but the rapid
effusions of a man immersed in business, contesting popu-
lous boroughs, sitting up half the night in Parliament,
passing estimates connected with his office, and making
speeches on *la haute politique* to the Commons of England. Mr. Gladstone, who remembers the splendour of
his early fame, does justice to the "immense distinction"
which Macaulay had attained long before middle life, and
justly remarks that, except the second Pitt and Lord
Byron, no Englishman had ever won, at so early an age,
such wide and honourable renown.

And behind this renown, unknown to the world, but
more honourable than the renown itself, were facts which
must for ever embalm Macaulay's memory with a fragrance

of lofty and unselfish virtue. The Whig Government, bent
on economy, brought in a bill to reform the Bankruptcy
jurisdiction. He voted for the measure, though it suppressed his Commissionership, and left him penniless ; for
at about the time his Trinity fellowship also expired. He
was reduced to such straits that he was forced to sell the
gold medals he had won at Cambridge ; and, as he said
at a later date, he did not know where to turn for a morsel
of bread. This did not last long, and his appointment to
the Board of Control, placed him in relative comfort. But
presently a new difficulty arose. The Government introduced their Slavery Bill ; which, though a liberal proposal,
did not satisfy the fanatics of the abolitionist party, among
whom Zachary Macaulay stood in the first rank. His son
made up his mind in a moment. He declared to his
colleagues and his chiefs that he could not go counter
to his father. "He has devoted his whole life to the
question ; and I cannot grieve him by giving way, when
he wishes me to stand firm." He placed his resignation
in the hands of Lord Althorp, and freely criticized as an
independent member the measure of his own Government. He told his leader that he did not expect such
insubordination to be overlooked ; and that if he were a
Minister he would not allow it. Such noble independence
had its reward. He wrote to his sister Hannah : " I have
resigned my office, and my resignation has been refused.
I have spoken and voted against the Ministry under
which I hold my place. . . . I am as good friends with
the Ministers as ever." Well might Sydney Smith say,
that Macaulay was incorruptible.

Still the *res angusta domi* was pressing hard upon—not
so much himself as his family, of which he was now the
main support. With his official salary, and with what

he earned by writing for the *Edinburgh*—which, by the way, never seems to have exceeded two hundred pounds per annum—he was beyond the pressure of immediate want.   If he had been out of office and at leisure, he, no doubt, would have gained far more by his pen.   But, as he pointedly put it, he was resolved to write only because his mind was full—not because his pockets were empty.   He accepted the post of legal adviser to the Supreme Council of India, from which he was sure to return with some twenty thousand pounds, saved out of his salary.   In his position it is difficult, even judging after the event, to say that he could have acted more wisely and prudently than he did.   But the sacrifice was great—and probably he knew it as well as any one, though with his usual cheery stoicism he said nothing about it.   The exile from England, and even removal from English politics, were probably a gain.   But the postponement of his monumental work in literature was a serious misfortune.   The precious hours of health and vigour were speeding away, and the great work was not begun, nor near beginning. He sailed for Madras, February 15, 1834.

He spent the time during his voyage in a very characteristic manner, by reading all the way.   " Except at meals," he said, " I hardly exchanged a word with any human being.   I devoured Greek, Latin, Spanish, Italian, French, and English ; folios, quartos, octavos, duodecimos."   He always had an immoderate passion for reading, on which he never seems to have thought of putting the slightest restraint.   When in India he writes to his sister, Mrs. Cropper, saying that he would like nothing so well as to bury himself in some great library, and never pass a waking hour without a book before him.   And as a matter of fact, except when engaged in business or com-

position this seems to have been what he actually did.
He walked about London, reading; he roamed through
the lanes of Surrey, reading; and even the new and surprising spectacle of the sea—so suggestive of reverie and
brooding thought—could not seduce him from his books.
His appetite was so keen as to be almost undiscriminating.
He was constantly reading worthless novels which he
despised. Once he is shocked himself, and exclaims in
his diary: "Why do I read such trash?" One would
almost say that his mind was naturally vacant when left
to itself, and needed the thoughts of others to fill up the
void. How otherwise are we to account for the following
extraordinary statement, under his own hand? He was
on a journey to Ireland :—

I read between London and Bangor the lives of the emperors
from Maximin to Carinus, inclusive, in the Augustan history.
. . . . We sailed as soon as we got on board. I put on my great
coat and sate on deck during the whole voyage. *As I could not
read*, I used an excellent substitute for reading. I went through
Paradise Lost in my head. I could still repeat half of it,
and that the best half.

The complaint is that Macaulay's writings lack meditation and thoughtfulness. Can it be wondered at, when
we see the way in which he passed his leisure hours.
One would have supposed that an historian and statesman, sailing for Ireland in the night on that Irish
sea, would have been visited by thoughts too full and
bitter and mournful to have left him any taste even for
the splendours of Milton's verse. He was about to write
on Ireland and the battle of the Boyne; and he had got
up the subject with his usual care before starting. Is it
not next to incredible that he could have thought of any-

thing else than that pathetic, miserable, humiliating story
of the connexion between the two islands? And he
knew that story better than most men. Yet it did not
kindle his mind on such an occasion as this. There was
a defect of deep sensibility in Macaulay—a want of moral
draught and earnestness, which is characteristic of his
writing and thinking. His acute intellect and nimble
fancy are not paired with an emotional endowment of
corresponding weight and volume. His endless and
aimless reading was the effect, not the cause, of this disposition. While in India he read more classics in one year
than a Cambridge undergraduate who was preparing to
compete for the Chancellor's medals.[5] But this incessant
reading was directed by no aim, to no purpose—was
prompted by no idea on which he wished to throw light,
no thoughtful conception which needed to be verified and
tested. Macaulay's omnivorous reading is often referred
to as if it were a title to honour; it was far more of
the nature of a defect. It is, by the way, a curious circumstance, that while on the one hand we are always told
of his extraordinary memory, insomuch that he only
needed to read a passage even once casually, for it to be

---

[5] " I have cast up my reading account, and brought it to the
end of 1835. It includes December, 1834. During the last thirteen,
months I have read Æschylus twice, Sophocles twice, Euripides
once, Pindar twice, Callimachus, Apollonius Rhodius, Quintus
Calaber, Theocritus twice, Herodotus, Thucydides, almost all
Xenophon's works, almost all Plato, Aristotle's *Politics*, and a good
deal of his *Organon*, besides dipping elsewhere in him, the whole
of Plutarch's *Lives*, about half of Lucian, two or three books of
Athenæus, Plautus twice, Terence twice, Lucretius twice, Ca-
tullus, Tibullus, Propertius, Lucan, Statius, Silius Italicus, Livy,
Velleius Paterculus, Sallust, Cæsar, and lastly Cicero. I have,
indeed, still a little of Cicero left, but I shall finish him in a few
days. I am now deep in Aristophanes and Lucian."

impressed on his mind for ever afterwards, on the other we
find that he read the same books over and over again, and
that at very short intervals. In the reading account just
given we see that he read several authors twice in one
year. But I happen to possess a copy of Lysias, which
belonged to him, which shows that he carried the practice
much further. He had the excellent habit of marking in
pencil the date of his last perusal of an author, and in the
book referred to, it appears that he read the speech
Pro Cæde Eratosthenis three times within a year, and
five times altogether ; and with most of the speeches
it was the same, though that one appears to have
been his favourite. In September and October, 1837,
he appears to have read all Lysias through twice over.
Now what could be the meaning or the motive of these
repeated perusals ? In the case of a man with a wretched
memory, who was about to undergo an examination, we
could understand them. But Macaulay's memory bordered on the miraculous, and he only read to please
himself. It seems very strange that a serious man should
thus dispose of his spare moments. How dry the
inward spring of meditation must have been to
remotely allow of such an employment of time ! That a
finished scholar however busy should now and then
solace himself with a Greek play or a few books of
Homer would only show that he had kept open the
windows of his mind, and had not succumbed to the dusty
drudgery of life. But this was not Macaulay's case.
He read with the ardour of a professor compiling a
lexicon, without a professor's object or valid motive.
He wanted a due sense of the relative importance of
books and studies.

It behoves a critic to be cautious in finding fault with

Macaulay, as he generally will discover that before he has done blaming him for one thing, he has to begin praising him warmly for another. His career in India is an instance in point. However excessive his taste for reading may have been, he never allowed that or any other private inclination to interfere with the practical work which lay before him. In Calcutta, as in London, he showed the same power of strenuous, unremitting labour, which never seemed to know satiety or fatigue. Besides his official duties as Member of Council, he at once assumed, voluntarily and gratuitously, an enormous addition to his burden of work by becoming chairman of two important committees : the Committee of Public Instruction and the committee appointed to draw up the new codes — the Penal Code and the Code of Criminal Procedure. He rarely failed to arrogate to himself the lion's share of any hard work within his reach. But on this occasion, owing to the frequent illness of his colleagues, he had at times to undertake the greater part of the task himself. The Penal Code and the notes appended to it are perhaps one of his most durable titles to fame. On such a subject I can have no opinion ; but this is the way in which Mr. Justice Stephen speaks of it :—

Lord Macaulay's great work was too daring and original to be accepted at once. It was a draft when he left India in 1838. The draft . . . and the revision (by Sir Barnes Peacock) are both eminently creditable to their authors, and the result of their successive efforts has been to reproduce in a concise and even beautiful form the spirit of the law of England. . . . . The point which always has surprised me most in connexion with the Penal Code is, that it proves that Lord Macaulay must have had a knowledge of English criminal law which, considering how little he had practised it, may fairly be called extraordi-

nary. He must have possessed the gift of going at once to the
very root of the matter, and of sifting the corn from the chaff,
to a most unusual degree, for his draft gives the substance of the
criminal law of England down to its minute working details, in
a compass which by comparison with the original may be
regarded as almost ludicrously small. The Indian Penal Code
is to the English criminal law what a manufactured article ready
for use is to the materials out of which it is made. It is to the
French Code Pénal, and I may add the North German Code of
1871, what a finished picture is to a sketch. It is far simpler
and much better expressed than Livingstone's Code of Louisiana,
and its practical success has been complete. The clearest proof
of this is, that hardly any questions have arisen upon it which
have had to be determined by the Courts, and that few and
slight amendments have had to be made by the Legislature.[6]

---

[6] *Trevelyan*, vol. i. cap. 6. Macaulay's labours on the Penal
Code, the value of which no one disputes, are sometimes spoken of
in a way which involves considerable injustice to his fellow-com-
missioners, whose important share in the work is tacitly ignored.
The Penal Code, together with the Report and Notes, are often
referred to as if they were Macaulay's exclusive work. For this
assumption there is no ground, and Macaulay himself never laid
claim to anything of the kind. When the illness of his colleagues
deprived him temporarily of their assistance he naturally mentioned the fact in his familiar correspondence; but this does not
justify the conclusion that he did all the work himself. Serious
as were the interruptions caused by the illness of the other com-
missioners, they were the exceptions, not the rule. Before the
rainy season of the year 1836 the Commission had been in full
work for a whole year, and nothing is said as to sickness during
all that time. Moreover, even when suffering from bad health,
Sir John Macleod maintained on the subject of their joint labours
daily communication with Macaulay, who submitted all he wrote
to the criticism of his friend, and repeated modifications of the
first draft were the result. This being so, it is not easy to see the
equity of calling the Penal Code " Macaulay's great work," as Sir
James Stephen does, or why the Report and Notes should appear
in the Library edition of Macaulay's writings.

On the Education Committee he rendered perhaps equal service, though it may not be so generally known. The members of the Board were evenly divided as to the character of the instruction to be given to the natives. Five were for continuing the old encouragement of Oriental learning, and five for the introduction of English literature and European science. It is hardly necessary to say into which scale Macaulay threw his influence. The opinion of the Government was determined by an elaborate minute which he drew up on the subject, and Lord William Bentinck decided that "the great object of the British Government ought to be the promotion of European literature and science among the natives of India."

Macaulay was very unpopular with a portion of the English residents in Calcutta, chiefly it would seem in consequence of a useful reform which he helped to introduce, affecting the jurisdiction of the provincial courts of Bengal. The change appears to have been a wise one, and generally accepted as such. But it was unfavourable to certain interests in the capital, and these attacked Macaulay in the press with the most scurrilous and indecent virulence. The foulness of the abuse was such that he could not allow the papers to lie in his sister's drawing-room. Cheat, swindler, charlatan, and tyrant were only the milder epithets with which he was assailed, and a suggestion to lynch him made at a public meeting was received with rapturous applause. He bore this disgraceful vituperation with the most unruffled equanimity. He did more : he vigorously advocated and supported the freedom of the press at the very moment when it was attacking him with the most rancorous invective. Macaulay had in him a vein of genuine magnanimity.

His period of exile in India drew to its close at the end of the year 1837. In the midst of his official work and multifarious reading he had written two articles for the *Edinburgh Review*, one on Mackintosh's *History of the Revolution;* the other his rather too famous Essay on Bacon. He made his plans for learning German on the voyage home. "People tell me that it is a hard language," he wrote to his friend Ellis, "but I cannot easily believe that there is a language which I cannot master in four months by working ten hours a day." He did learn German in the time prescribed ; but except to read Goethe and Schiller and parts of Lessing, he never seems to have made much use of it. However, his object in going to India was now attained. He had realized a modest fortune, but ample for his simple wants and tastes. After an unusually long voyage he reached England in the middle of the year 1838. His father had died while he was on the ocean.

Within a few weeks he had contributed to the *Edinburgh Review* one of the best of his essays, that on Sir William Temple. In October he left England for a tour in Italy.

The first visit to Italy is always an epoch in the life of a cultivated mind. Probably few pilgrims to the classic land were ever better prepared than Macaulay by reading and turn of thought to receive the unique impressions of such a journey. He was equally capable of appreciating both the antiquities, the Pagan and the Christian, of which Italy is the guardian. Fortunately he kept a journal of his travels, from which a few extracts have been published. They show Macaulay in his most attractive and engaging mood. A want of reverence for the men of genius of past ages is not one of the sins which lies at his door.

On the contrary, after family affection it was perhaps
the strongest emotion of his mind. He now had an
opportunity of indulging it such as he had never had
before. Here are a few extracts from his journal :—

Florence, November 9, 1838.—To the Church of Santa Croce
—an ugly, mean outside, and not much to admire in the architecture within " (shade of Mr. Ruskin !), "but consecrated by the
dust of some of the greatest men that ever lived. It was to me
what a first visit to Westminster Abbey would be to an American. The first tomb that caught my eye as I entered was that
of Michael Angelo. I was much moved, and still more so when,
going forward, I saw the stately monument lately erected to
Dante. The figure of the poet seemed to me fine, and finely
placed, and the inscription very happy—his own words—the pro-
clamation which resounds through the shades when Virgil
returns :—

> Onorate l'altissimo poeta.

The two allegorical figures were not much to my taste. It is
particularly absurd to represent Poetry weeping for Dante. . . .
Yet I was very near shedding tears of a different kind as I looked
at this magnificent monument, and thought of the sufferings of
the great poet, and of his incomparable genius, and of all the
pleasure which I have derived from him, and of his death in exile,
and of the late justice of posterity. I believe that very few
people have ever had their minds more thoroughly penetrated
with the spirit of any great work than mine is with that of the
Divine Comedy. His execution I take to be far beyond that
of any other artist who has operated on the imagination by
means of words—

> O degli altri poeti onore e lume
> Vagliami il lungo studio e 'l grande amore
> Che m' han fatto cercar lo tuo volume.

I was proud to think that I had a right to apostrophize him
thus. I went on, and next I came to the tomb of Alfieri. I

D

passed forward, and in another minute my foot was on the grave
of Machiaveli.

At Rome he is almost overpowered.

November 18.—On arriving this morning I walked straight
from the hotel door to St. Peter's. I was so excited by the expec-
tation of what I was to see that I could notice nothing else. I
was quite nervous. The colonnade in front is noble—very, very
noble; yet it disappointed me, and would have done so had it
been the portico of Paradise. In I went. I was for a minute
fairly stunned by the magnificence and harmony of the interior.
I never in my life saw, and never, I suppose, shall see again, anything so astonishingly beautiful. I really could have cried with
pleasure. I rambled about for half an hour or more, paying
little or no attention to details, but enjoying the effect of the
sublime whole.

In rambling back to the Piazza di Spagna I found myself
before the portico of the Pantheon. I was as much struck and
affected as if I had not known that there was such a building
in Rome. There it was, the work of the age of Augustus—the
work of men who lived with Cicero and Cæsar, and Horace and
Virgil.

He never seems to have felt annoyed, as some have
been, by the intermingling of Christian and Pagan Rome,
and is at a loss to say which interested him most. He
was already meditating his essay on the history of the
Popes, and throwing into his *Lays of Ancient Rome* those
geographical and topographical touches which set his
spirited stanzas ringing in the ear of a traveller in Rome
at every turn.

I then went to the river, to the spot where the old Pons Sub-
licius stood, and looked about to see how my *Horatius* agreed
with the topography. Pretty well; but his house must be on
Mount Palatine, for he could never see Mount Cœlius from
the spot where he fought.

But like all active minds to whom hard work has
become a habit, Macaulay soon grew weary of the idleness
of travelling.   He never went further south than Naples,
and turned away from the Campagna, leaving the delights
of an Italian spring untasted, to seek his labour and his
books at home.   He reached London early in February,
1839, and fell to work with the eager appetite of a man
who has had a long fast.   In less than three weeks he
had read and reviewed Mr. Gladstone's book on *Church
and State*.   But he was not destined to enjoy his leisure
long.   The expiring Whig Ministry of Lord Melbourne
needed all the support they could obtain : he was brought
into Parliament as member for Edinburgh, and soon after
admitted into the Cabinet as Secretary-at-War.

This return to office and Parliament was an uncom-
pensated loss to literature, and no gain to politics.   The
Whig Ministry was past saving ; and Macaulay could
gain no distinction by fighting their desperate battle.   He
felt himself that he was wasting his time.   " I pine,"
he wrote, " for liberty and ease, and freedom of speech
and freedom of pen."   For this political interlude had
necessitated the laying aside of his History, which he had
already begun.   He had now reached an age at which an
author who meditates a great work has no time to lose.
He was just turned forty ; a judicious economy of his time
and resources would have seen him a long way towards
the performance of the promise with which his great work
opens,—" I purpose to write the history of England from
the accession of King James II. down to a time which is
within the memory of men still living."   It is impossible
to read the forecast he made of his work on the eve of
his journey to Italy without a pang of regret, and sense of
a loss not easily estimated.

As soon as I return I shall seriously commence my History. The first part (which I think will take up five octavo volumes) will extend from the Revolution to the commencement of Sir Robert Walpole's long administration—a period of three-or-four-and-thirty very eventful years. From the commencement of Walpole's administration to the commencement of the American war, events may be despatched more concisely. From the commencement of the American war it will again become necessary to be copious. How far I shall bring the narrative down I have not determined. The death of George IV. would be the best halting place.

It was all in his mind. He had gone over the ground again and again. What a panorama he would have unfolded! what battle-pieces we should have had of Marlborough's campaigns! what portraits of Bolingbroke, Peterborough, Prince Eugene, and the rest! It is a sad pity that Lord Melbourne, who was fond of letting things alone, could not leave Macaulay alone, but must needs yoke the celestial steed to his parliamentary plough. Or, to put it more fairly, it is a pity that Macaulay himself had not sufficient nerve, and consciousness of his mission, to resist the tempter. But he was loyal to a degree of chivalry to his political friends who were in difficulties. He was, as his sister's writing-master said, a "lump of good nature;" and without a full consciousness of the sacrifice he was making, he gave up to party what was meant for literature.

But he had a parliamentary triumph of no common kind—one of the two instances in which, as Mr. Gladstone says, "he arrested the successful progress of legislative measures, and slew them at a moment's notice, and by his single arm." The case was Sergeant Talfourd's Copyright Bill. His conduct on this occasion has been strangely questioned by Miss Martineau, who wonders how an able literary man could utter such a speech, and hints "at some cause which could not be alleged for such a man exposing himself in a speech unsound in its whole argument." In any case, Macaulay had much more to lose by the line he took than Miss Martineau. No one, we may suppose at present, can read the oration in question without entire conviction of the single-minded sense of duty and elevated public spirit which animated him on this occasion. Nothing can be more judicial than the way in which he balances the respective claims to consideration of authors and the general public. In the following year he had a similar victory over Lord Mahon; and the present law of copyright was framed in accordance with his proposals, slightly modified. Macaulay made a most advantageous contrast to his brother authors in this matter. Even the "writer of books" who petitioned from Chelsea showed that he had considered the subject to much less purpose.

Lord Melbourne's Government fell in June 1841; and the general election which followed gave the Tories a crushing majority. Macaulay was freed from "that closely watched slavery which is mocked with the name of power." He welcomed the change with exuberant delight. He still retained his seat for Edinburgh, and spoke occasionally in the House; but he was liberated from the wasteful drudgery of office.

Here it will be well to interrupt this personal sketch of the writer, and proceed to a consideration of some of his work. But for the purpose of making clear some allusions in the two following chapters, we may state in anticipation that he had a serious attack of illness in the year 1852, from which he never entirely recovered.

CHAPTER II.

CHARACTERISTICS.

MACAULAY belongs to a class of writers whom critics do not always approach with sufficient circumspection and diffidence, the class, namely, of writers whose merits and defects appear to be so obvious that there is no mistaking them. When dealing with writers of this kind, we are apt to think our task much easier and simpler than it really is. Writers of startling originality and depth, difficult as it may be to appraise them justly, yet, as it were, warn critics to be on their guard and take their utmost pains. Lesser writers, again, but of odd and peculiar flavour, are nearly sure of receiving adequate attention. But there are writers who belong to neither of these classes, whose merit consists neither in profound originality nor special flavour, but in a general wide eloquence and power, coupled with a certain commonplaceness of thought, of whom Cicero may be taken as the supreme type, and by those writers critics are liable to be deceived—in two ways. Either they admire the eloquence so much that they are blind to other deficiencies, or they perceive the latter so clearly that they fail to do justice to the other merits. On no writer have more opposite judgments been passed than on Cicero. By some he has been regarded as one of the loftiest geniuses of antiquity ; by others as a shallow, verbose, and ignorant pretender; and perhaps to this day Cicero's exact position in literature has not been settled. It is to be hoped that Macaulay, who has a certain distant resemblance to Cicero, will not be so long in finding his proper place.

That something like a reaction against Macaulay's fame has recently set in, can hardly be doubted. It was, indeed, to be expected that something of the kind would occur. Such reactions against the fame of great authors frequently appear in the generation which follows the period of their first splendour. New modes of thought and sentiment arise, amid which the celebrity of a recent past appears old-fashioned, with little of the grace which clothes the genuinely old. We cannot be surprised if a fate which overtook Pope, Voltaire, and Byron, should now overtake Macaulay. But those writers have risen anew into the firmament of literature, from which they are not likely to fall again. The question is, whether Macaulay will ultimately join them as a fixed star, and if so, of what magnitude? It would be against analogy if such a wide and resonant fame as his were to suffer permanent eclipse. Hasty reputations, due to ephemeral circumstances, may utterly die out, but it would not be easy to name a really great fame among contemporaries which has not been largely ratified by posterity. Few authors have had greater contemporary fame than Macaulay. It spread through all classes and countries like an epidemic. Foreign courts and learned societies vied with the multitude in doing him honour. He was read with almost equal zest in cultivated European capitals and in the scattered settlements of remote colonies. The Duke of Wellington was loud in his praise. Professor Ranke called him an incomparable man: and a body of English workmen sent him a vote of thanks for having

written a history which working men could understand.
An author who collects suffrages from such opposite
quarters as these must have had the secret of touching a
deep common chord in human nature. It is the business
of criticism to find out what that chord was.

Macaulay's great quality is that of being one of the
best story-tellers that ever lived ; and if we limit the
competition to his only proper rivals—the historians—
he may be pronounced *the* best story-teller. If any one
thinks these superlatives misplaced, let him mention the
historical writers whom he would put on a level with or
above Macaulay—always remembering that the comparison
is limited to this particular point : the art of telling a
story with such interest and vivacity that readers have
no wish but to read on. If the area of comparison be
enlarged so as to include questions of intellectual depth,
moral insight, and sundry other valuable qualities, the
competition turns against Macaulay, who at once sinks
many degrees in the scale. But in his own line he has no
rival. And let no one undervalue that line. He kindled
a fervent human interest in past and real events which
novelists kindle in fictitious events. He wrote of the
seventeenth century with the same vivid sense of present
reality which Balzac and Thackeray had, when they wrote
of the nineteenth century, which was before their eyes
And this was the peculiarity which fascinated contemporaries, and made them so lavish of praise and admiration.
They felt, and very justly, that history had never been so
written before. It was a quality which all classes, of all
degrees of culture, could almost equally appreciate. But it
produced a feeling of gratitude among the more experienced
judges which seems likely to pass away. All the younger
generation who have grown to manhood since Macaulay

wrote, have become intimately acquainted with his writings
at too early an age to appreciate what an innovator he was
in his day.   Besides, he has had numerous able though
inferior imitators.   The younger folk therefore see nothing
surprising that history should be made as entertaining as a
novel.   But twenty or thirty years ago the case was very
different.   Lord Carlisle when he finished the fifth (posthumous) volume, said he was "in despair to close that brilliant-
pictured page."   It will generally be found that old men
who were not far from being Macaulay's equals in age, are
still enthusiastic in his praise.   It is the younger generation, who have come to maturity since his death, who see a
good deal to censure in him, and not very much to admire.
The late Sir James Stephen said "he could forgive him
anything, and was violently tempted to admire even his
faults."   Mr. Leslie Stephen, his son, is one of the most
penetrating and severe of Macaulay's critics.

There is evidently a misunderstanding here which needs
removing.   It is another instance of the opposite sides of
the shield producing discrepant opinions as to its colour.
Those who admire Macaulay, and those who blame him, are
thinking of different things.   His admirers are thinking
of certain brilliant qualities in which he has hardly ever
been surpassed.   His censors, passing these by with hasty
recognition, point to grave defects, and ask if such are
compatible with real greatness.   Each party should be
led to adopt part of his opponent's view, without surren-
dering what is true in his own.   Macaulay's eminence as
a *raconteur* should not only be admitted with cold assent,
but proclaimed supreme and unrivalled in its own way,
as it really is.   On the other hand, his serious deficiencies
in other ways should be acknowledged with equal
frankness.

One of his most remarkable qualities as a writer is his power of interesting the reader and holding his attention. It is a gift by itself, and not very easy to analyze. Some of the greatest writers have wanted it.

Dr. Johnson, speaking of Prior's *Solomon* and the partiality with which its author regarded it, says,—

His affection was natural; it had undoubtedly been written with great labour, and who is willing to think that he has been labouring in vain? He had infused into it much knowledge and much thought; he had polished it often to elegance, and often dignified it with splendour, and sometimes heightened it to sublimity. He perceived in it many excellencies, and did not discover that it wanted that without which all others are of small avail—the power of engaging attention and alluring curiosity. Tediousness is the most fatal of faults.

Of the truth of this last remark there is no doubt. But what was the secret of the tediousness of the poem *Solomon*, which, according to Johnson, was almost as great a paragon as the Hebrew monarch afte whom it was named? A work on which great labour had been spent, which contained thought and knowledge, which had polish, elegance, splendour, and occasionally sublimity, one would have thought was not likely to be dull. As a matter of fact, *Solomon* is dead and buried fathoms deep in its own dulness. In this special case Johnson gives at least one good reason, but he throws no light on the general question of dulness—in what it consists, by which we might also explain in what interest consists. It appears that Macaulay himself was puzzled with the same difficulty. " Where lies," he asks somewhat unjustly, with reference to a novel of Lord Lytton, " the secret of being amusing? and how is it that art, eloquence, and diligence may all be employed in making a book dull?"

Few authors have had in larger degree than Macaulay "the secret of being amusing," of " engaging attention and alluring curiosity," as Dr. Johnson says. He is rarely, perhaps never, absolutely dull. On the other hand, he is not too lively and stimulating, and avoids therefore producing that sense of fatigue in the reader, which even genuine wit, if there is too much of it, is apt to engender. He had the talent which he concedes to Walpole, of writing what people like to read. Perhaps the secret of his charm lay in this : First that he was deeply interested himself in the subjects that he handles. His *bonâ fide* wish to do them justice—to impart his knowledge—is not hampered by any anxious self-consciousness as to the impression he himself is making. His manner is straightforward and frank, and therefore winning, and he communicates the interest he feels. Secondly, he was an adept in the art of putting himself *en rapport* with his reader—of not going too fast, or too far, or too deep, for the ordinary intelligence. He takes care not only to be clear in language, but to follow a line of thought from which obscurity and even twilight are excluded. His attention, indeed, to the needs of dull readers was excessive, and has risked the esteem of readers of another kind. He often steered too near the shoals of commonplace to suit the taste of many persons ; still he never fairly runs aground. He has one great merit which can be appreciated by all—his thought is always well within his reach, and is unfolded with complete mastery and ease to its uttermost filament. He is never vague, shadowy, and incomplete. The reader is never perplexed by ideas imperfectly grasped, by thoughts which the writer cannot fully express. On the other hand, his want of aspiration, of all effort to rise into the higher regions of thought, has

lost him in the opinion of many readers. He is one of
the most entertaining but also one of the least suggestive
of writers.

His powers of brilliant illustration have never been
denied, and it would not be easy to name their equal.
His command of perfectly apposite and natural, yet not at
all obvious images, is not more wonderful than the ease
with which they are introduced. Few readers are likely
to have forgotten the impression they once made on the
youthful mind. It was something quite new and almost
bewildering, like the first night at the play. He can
conjure up in a moment a long vista of majestic similes,
which attracts the eye like a range of snow-capped moun-
tains. Take, for instance, the opening passages of the
articles on *Lord Clive* and *Ranke's History of the Popes*.
As soon as the curtain rises, a grand panorama seems
spread out before us. The first begins with a comparison
between the English conquests of India, and the Spanish
conquest of America. But notice how pictorially it is
done :—

The people of India when we subdued them, were ten times
as numerous as the Americans whom the Spaniards vanquished,
and were at the same time quite as highly civilized as the vic-
torious Spaniards. They had reared cities larger and fairer than
Saragossa and Toledo, and buildings more beautiful and costly
than the Cathedral of Seville. They could show bankers richer
than the richest firms of Barcelona or Cadiz ; viceroys whose
splendour far surpassed that of Ferdinand the Catholic ; myriads
of cavalry and long trains of artillery which would have asto-
nished the Great Captain.

The passage is spoiled by mutilation ; but readers can
turn to it if they do not remember it. In the same way
the article on the Popes opens with a truly grand picture.

" No other institution " (save the Papacy) " is left stand-
ing which carries the mind back to the times when the
smoke of sacrifice rose from the Pantheon, and when
camelopards and tigers bounded in the Flavian Amphi-
theatre." Again : " She was great and respected before
the Saxon had set foot in Britain, before the Frank had
passed the Rhine, when Grecian eloquence still flourished
in Antioch, when idols were still worshipped in the
Temple of Mecca." The sensitive youth feels his breath
catch at illustrations like these. If they pall on the older
mind it is because they are found to be addressed almost
exclusively to the eye : they are followed by nothing of
importance addressed to the reason. We shall have occasion to see that this sumptuous opening of the article on
the Popes leads to a disquisition at once inaccurate in
facts and superficial in argument.

Macaulay's talent as an historical artist will be considered at some length when we come to examine the
History of England. It will be sufficient in this general
view to remark the skill with which he has overcome the
peculiar difficulties of historical composition. The great
difficulty in drawing the picture of a complex society
in a past age is to combine unity with breadth of composition. In a long narrative only a very small portion
of the picture can be seen at one time. The whole
is never presented at one moment with concentrated
effect, such as the painter can command, who places
on one canvas which can be easily surveyed, all that he
has to tell us. The historian cannot bring all his troops
on the ground at once and strike the mind by a wide and
magnificent display. He is reduced to a march past in
narrow file. The danger, therefore, is that the effect of
the whole will be feeble or lost. In the hands of a weak

man a thin stream of narrative meanders on, but a broad
view is nowhere obtained. The lowest form of historical
writing is the chronicle or mere annals, in which a broad
view is not so much as aimed at. In great historical
work, the immediate portion of the narrative passing
before the reader's eye is always kept in subordinate relation to the whole drama of which it forms a part. And
this is the problem, to keep the whole suggestively before
the reader while only a part is being shown. Only a
strong imagination is equal to this task. The mind of the
writer must hold the entire picture suspended in his fancy
while he is painting each separate portion of it. And he
paints each separate portion of it with a view to its fit-
ness and relation to the whole.

No fair critic will deny that Macaulay's execution in
all these respects is simply masterly. The two volumes
which comprise the reign of James II. in spite of their
abundant detail are as truly an organic whole as a
sonnet. Though the canvas is crowded in every part
with events and characters, there is no confusion, no
obstruction to clear vision. Wherever we stand we seem
to be opposite to the centre of the picture. However
interested we may be in a part, we are never allowed to
lose sight of the whole. The compelling force of the
writer's imagination always keeps it in a latent suggestive
way before our minds. And all this is done under a self-
imposed burden which is without example. For, in
obedience to his canon as to how history should be written,
the author has weighted himself with a load of minute
detail such as no historian ever uplifted before. He
hardly ever mentions a site, a town, a castle, a manor-
house, he rarely introduces even a subordinate character,
without bringing in a picturesque anecdote, an association,

a reminiscence out of his boundless stores of knowledge, which sparkles like a gem on the texture of his narrative. Nothing can exceed the skill with which these little vignettes are thrown in, and they are incessant ; yet they never seem to be in the way, or to hinder the main effect. Take as an instance this short reference to the Earl of Craven. It occurs in the very crisis of the story, when James II. was a prisoner in his own palace, between his first and second attempts to fly the country :—

James, while his fate was under discussion, remained at Whitehall, fascinated, as it seemed, by the greatness and nearness of the danger, and unequal to the exertion of either struggling or flying. In the evening news came that the Dutch had occupied Chelsea and Kensington. The king, however, prepared to go to rest as usual. The Coldstream Guards were on duty at the palace. They were commanded by William, Earl of Craven, an aged man, who, more than fifty years before, had been distinguished in war and love, who had led the forlorn hope at Creutznach with such courage that he had been patted on the shoulder by the great Gustavus, and who was believed to have won from a thousand rivals the heart of the unfortunate Queen of Bohemia. Craven was now in his eightieth year ; yet time had not tamed his spirit. It was past ten o'clock when he was informed that three battalions of the Prince's foot, mingled with some troops of horse, were pouring down the long avenue of St. James's Park, with matches lighted, and in full readiness for action. Count Solmes, who commanded the foreigners, said that his orders were to take military possession of the posts round Whitehall, and exhorted Craven to retire peaceably. Craven swore that he would rather be cut to pieces; but when the king, who was undressing himself, learned what was passing, he forbade the stout old soldier to attempt a resistance which must have been ineffectual.

How truly artistic ! and how much Craven's conduct is

explained and heightened by that little touch recalling
Creutznach, the forlorn hope, and the Great Gustavus!
What a vista up the seventeenth century to the far off
Thirty Years' War is opened in a moment! I recall no
writer who is Macaulay's equal in this art of covering his
larger surfaces with minute work which is never out of
place. Like the delicate sculpture on the sandals of
Athene in the Parthenon, it detracts nothing from the
grandeur of the statue. Or, to take a more appropriate
figure, it resembles a richly decorated Gothic porch, in
which every stone is curiously carved, and yet does its
duty in bearing the weight of the mighty arch as well as
if it were perfectly plain.

There are only two modern men with whom he can
be worthily compared, Michelet and Carlyle. Both are
his superiors in what Mr. Ruskin calls penetrative
imagination. Both have an insight into the moral world
and the mind of man, of which he is wholly incapable.
Both have a simple directness of vision, the real poet's
eye for nature and character, which he entirely lacks.
Carlyle especially can emit a lightning flash, which
makes Macaulay's prose, always a little pompous in his
ambitious flights, burn dim and yellow. But on another
side Macaulay has his revenge. For clear broad width, for
steadiness of view and impartiality of all-round presentation he is their superior. Carlyle's dazzling effects
of white light are frequently surrounded by the blackest
gloom. Even that lovely "evening sun of July"—in a
well-known passage of the *French Revolution*—emerges
only for a moment from a dark cloud, which speedily
obscures it again. Michelet's light is less fitful than
Carlyle's; it is perhaps also less brilliant. Macaulay's
light, pale in comparison with their meteoric splendours,

has the advantage of being equal and steady, and free from the danger of going out. There is yet another quality in which he gains by comparison with the strongest men—the art of historical perspective. His scenes are always placed at the right distance for taking in their full effect. The vividness of Carlyle's imagination often acts like a powerful telescope, and brings objects too near the observer. The events in the French Revolution very often appear as if enacted under our windows. What is just in front of us we see with almost oppressive distinctness, but the eye cannot range over a wide yet perfectly visible panorama. Macaulay never falls into this error. His pictures are always far enough off for the whole sweep of the prospect to be seen with ease. He seems to lead us up to a lofty terrace overlooking a spacious plain which lies spread out below. For size, power, and brightness, if not always purity of colour, he has some title to be called the Rubens of historians.

Admitting all, or a portion, of what is thus advanced, the opposition to Macaulay has a very serious counter-statement to offer. The chief complaint—and it is sufficiently grave—is of a constant and pervading want of depth, either of thought or sentiment. Macaulay, it is said, did little or nothing to stir the deeper mind or the deeper feelings of his multitude of readers.

As regards the first charge, want of intellectual depth, it is not easy to imagine even the semblance of a defence. Indeed, Macaulay owns his guilt with a certain amount of bravado. He has expressed his contempt of all higher speculation with too much scorn to leave any room for doubt or apology on that head. He never refers to Philosophy except in a tone of disparagement and sneer. " Such speculations are in a peculiar manner the delight

E

of intelligent children and half-civilized men." Among
the speculations thus dismissed with derision are the
questions of "the necessity of human actions and the
foundation of moral obligation." Thus Macaulay disbelieved in the possibility of ethical science. Of a
translation of Kant which had been sent him he speaks
with amusing airs of superiority, says he cannot understand a word of it any more than if it had been written
in Sanscrit; fully persuaded that the fault lay with Kant,
and not with himself. But his dislike of arduous thinking
did not stop with philosophy. He speaks of Montesquieu
with great disdain; pronounces him to be specious, but
obscure as an oracle, and shallow as a Parisian coxcomb.
There is no trace in Macaulay's writings or life that he was
ever arrested by an intellectual difficulty of any kind. He
can bombard with great force of logic and rhetoric an
enemy's position; but his mind never seems to have
suggested to him problems of its own. In reading him
we glide along the smoothest surface, we are hurried from
picture to picture, but we never meet with a thoughtful
pause which makes us consider with closed eyes what the
conclusion may well be. Strange to say, he more nearly
approaches discussion of principles in his speeches than in
other portions of his works : but a writer of less speculative force hardly exists in the language. It is not easy
to see from his diaries and correspondence that he had any
intellectual interests of any kind, except his taste—if that
can be called an intellectual interest—for poetry, and the
Greek and Latin classics. His letters are, with few exceptions, mere lively gossip. He rarely discusses even
politics, in which he took so large a share, with any
serious heartiness.[1] He just gives the last news. He does

[1] The only even apparent exceptions to this general statement

not betray the slightest interest in science, or social or religious questions, except an amusing petulance at the progress of the Tractarian movement, on which he writes squibs : but otherwise he lived in almost complete isolation amid the active intellectual life of his day. He appears to have been almost wholly wanting in intellectual curiosity of any kind.

This is shown by the strange indifference with which he treated his own subject—history. He lived in an age in which some of the most important historical works that the world has ever seen, were published. He was contemporary (to name only the chief) with Sismondi, De Barante, Guizot, the two Thierrys, Mignet, Michelet, in France; with Raumer, Schlosser, Niebuhr, Otfried, Müller, Gans, Neander, F. G. Bauer, Waitz, Roth, in Germany. He never mentions one of them—except Sismondi with a sneer. The only modern historians of whom he takes notice are Ranke and Hallam—and this not with a view to considering the value of their historical work proper, but because they furnished him with a convenient armoury for his own polemical purposes. If he had had any wide generous interest in the progress of historical knowledge, he must have shown more sympathy with men engaged in the same field of labour as himself. He professed to be a

---

is a group of four or five letters of the year 1845, recounting Lord John Russell's abortive attempt to form a ministry; and a truly admirable letter to Mr. Ellis, narrating the scene in the House of Commons on the passing of the first Reform Bill by a majority of one. But even these letters deal chiefly with news, and hardly attempt the discussion of principles.

Perhaps the time has not yet come for a fully representative selection of Macaulay's best letters. He must have written, one would think, to his colleagues and others with more weight and earnestness than appears anywhere at present.

reformer of history. These men were reformers who had proclaimed, and put in practice, every principle of any value which he advocated in the *Edinburgh Review*, in his article on History, published in 1828. He lays down, not without a certain air as of a discoverer, the new method on which he conceives history should be written—that it should be not abstract and logical, but concrete, graphic, and picturesque. One might have expected that two of the most picturesque presentations of past times which literature has to show, which, when Macaulay wrote his article, had been recently published and attracted European attention, would have been at least named on such an occasion. De Barante's *Histoire des Ducs de Bourgogne* (published in 1824-26), and Augustin Thierry's *Histoire de la Conquête d'Angleterre par les Normands* (1825), had a success in the world of letters second only to Macaulay's own success some quarter of a century later with his *History of England*. Those writers were busy with the very task which he summoned historians to take in hand. Their fame was recent and prominent, one of the events of the day. He was writing on a subject from which a reference to them, one would think, could not be excluded. It is excluded, as completely as if they had never existed. How may this be explained? Did he not know their works? or did he not appreciate them? Neither alternative is welcome. His friend Hallam, when an old man worn down with years and domestic afflictions, set him a very different example. In his supplementary volume to the *History of the Middle Ages*, he shows how carefully he had made himself acquainted with all the more important historical inquiries of the Continent. But then, Hallam cared for the progress of historical research: he saw that history was full of problems which required

solution. He *could* not be indifferent to what other men
were doing. It is to be feared that Macaulay cared for
little besides his own success as an historical artist.

The most important reform in historical studies ever
made, has been the application of a critical method to the
study of the past ; in other words, the application of as
much of scientific carefulness and precision as the subject
allows.   This revolution—for it is nothing less—had
already begun in Macaulay's youth : and during his life-
time it had won notable victories in almost every field of
historical inquiry.   He not only did nothing for historical
criticism, he does not seem to have been aware of its
existence.   He took as little notice of the labours of his
countrymen, Palgrave, Dr. Guest, Kemble, as he did of
the labours of foreigners.   He investigated no obscure
questions, cleared up no difficulties, reversed the opinion
of scholars upon no important point.   The following passage in a letter to his friend Ellis is characteristic :
" While I was reading the earlier books (of Livy), I went
again through Niebuhr ; and I am sorry to say, that
having always been a little sceptical about his merits, I
am now a confirmed unbeliever "—a judgment which
throws more light on Macaulay's own merits than on
Niebuhr's.

The want of ethical depth is at least as striking.   He
looks away from moral problems, even more resolutely
than from intellectual problems.   He never has anything
to say on the deeper aspects and relations of life , and it
would not be easy to quote a sentence from either his
published works or private letters which shows insight
or meditation on love, or marriage, or friendship, or the
education of children, on religious faith or doubt.   We
find no trace in him of a " wise spirit," which has had

practical experience of the solemn realities and truths of
existence. His learning is confined to book-lore : he is
not well read in the human heart, and still less in the
human spirit. His unspirituality is complete ; we never
catch " a glimpse of the far land" through all his
brilliant narratives ; never, in his numerous portraits,
comes a line of moral suggestiveness, showing an eye
for the deeper springs of character, the finer shades of
motive. His inability to criticize works of poetry and
fiction extended to their chief subject—the human heart ;
and it may be noticed that the remarkable interest he
often awakens in a story which he tells so admirably, is
nearly always the interest of adventure, never the interest
of psychological analysis. Events and outward actions are
told with incomparable clearness and vigour—but a thick
curtain hangs before the inward theatre of the mind,
which is never revealed on his stage. He had a favourite
theory on which he often insisted, that children were the
only true poets : and this, because of the vividness of
their impressions. "No man, whatever his sensibility
may be, is ever affected by Hamlet, or Lear, as a little girl
is affected by the story of poor little Red Riding-hood,"
—as if the *force* of the impression were everything, and
its *character* nothing. By this rule, wax-work should be
finer art than the best sculpture in stone. The impressiveness of remote suggestive association by which high
art touches the deepest chords of feeling, Macaulay,
apparently, did not recognize. He had no ear for the finer
harmonies of the inner life.

The truth is that he almost wholly lacked the
stronger passions. A sweet affectionate tenderness for
friends and relations was the deepest emotion he knew.
This, coupled with his unselfishness, made him a most

winning character to those near him, as it certainly
filled his life with placid content and happiness. But
there is no evidence of strong feeling in his story.
I cannot readily believe the report that he was ever at
one time a good hater. He had his tempers of course,
like other men; but what sign is there of any fervent
heat, or lasting mood of passion ? Even in politics—the
side on which he was most susceptible of strong feeling—
he soon became calm, reasonable, gentle—like the good,
upright, amiable man he was. Consider his prudence.
He never took a hasty or unwise step in his life. His
judgment was never misled in matters of conduct for
a single moment. He walked in the honourable path he
had chosen with a certainty as unerring as if Minerva had
been present at his side. He never seems to have had
occasion either to yield to, or to resist, a strong temptation.
He was never in love. Ambition never got possession of
his mind. We cannot imagine him doing anything wrong,
or even indecorous : an elopement, a duel, an esclandre of
any kind, cannot be associated even in imagination with
his name. He was as blameless as Telemachus—

> Centred in the sphere
> Of common duties, decent not to fail
> In offices of tenderness, and pay
> Meet adoration to the household gods,

of spotless respectability. He is not to be blamed, but
very much envied, for such a constitution of mind. But
this is not the stuff of which great writers who stir men's
hearts are made. He makes us esteem him so much that
we can do little more ; he cannot provoke our love, pity,
or passionate sympathy. There is no romance, pathos,
or ideality in his life or his writings. We never leave him

conscious that we have been raised into a higher tone of
feeling, chastened and subdued into humility, courage, and
sacrifice.   He never makes us feel " what shadows we
are and what shadows we pursue."   How should he ?
His own view of life was essentially flat and prosaic.
Not an aspiration for the future ; no noble unrest and
discontent with the present ; no sympathetic tenderness
for the past.   He resembled Rubens in more ways than
one.

No phenomenon in the human mind (says Mr. Ruskin) is
more extraordinary than the junction of this cold worldly
temper with great rectitude of principle and tranquil kindness
of heart.   Rubens was an honourable and entirely well in-
tentioned man, earnestly industrious, simple and temperate in
habits of life, high-bred, learned, and discreet; his affection for
his mother was great; his generosity to contemporary artists
unfailing.   He is a healthy, worthy, kind-hearted, courtly-
phrased—animal, without any clearly perceptible traces of a
soul, except when he paints his children.[2]

Macaulay had no children of his own to paint : but no
man was ever fonder of children.

He was, beyond all comparison, the best of playfellows ; unrivalled in the invention of games, and never wearied of repeating them.   He had an inexhaustible repertory of small dramas
for the benefit of his nieces, in which he sustained an endless
number of parts. . . .   There was one never-failing game, of
building up a den with newspapers behind the sofa, and of enact-
ing robbers and tigers—the children shrieking with terror, but
always fascinated, and begging him to begin again.[3]

He had complete sympathy with children, and knew

    [2] *Modern Painters*, vol. v. part 9.
    [3] *Trevelyan*, vol. ii. cap. ii.

the way to their hearts better than to those of their seniors. Once he bought a superb sheet of paper for a guinea, on which to write a valentine to his little niece Alice. He notes in his diary on the 14th Feb.

> At three . . . came the children. Alice was in perfect raptures over her valentine. She begged quite pathetically to be told the truth about it. When we were alone together she said, "I am going to be very serious." Down she fell before me on her knees, and lifted up her hands: " Dear Uncle, do tell the truth to your little girl. Did you send the valentine ? " I did not choose to tell a real lie to a child, even about such a trifle, and so I owned it

A charming little scene, showing Macaulay's two best sides, tenderness and rectitude. But again; to distress, or its artful counterfeit, he was always pitiful and generous. In his journal he writes: " Dec. 27.—Disagreeable weather, and disagreeable news. —— is in difficulty again. I sent 50*l.*, and shall send the same to ——, who does not ask it. But I cannot help being vexed. All the fruits of my book have for this year been swallowed up. It will be all that I can do to make both ends meet without breaking in upon capital." Leigh Hunt enclosed in a begging letter a criticism on the *Roman Lays*, lamenting that they wanted the true poetical aroma which breathes from Spenser's *Faëry Queen*. Macaulay, who had none of an author's vanity, was " much pleased" with this sincerity.

Is there not reason to doubt whether a natural predisposition to the cardinal virtues is the best outfit for the prophet, the artist, or even the preacher ? Saints from of old have been more readily made out of publicans and sinners than out of Pharisees who pay tithes of all they possess. The artist, the writer and even the philosopher, equally need passion to do great work ; and genuine passion is ever apt to be unruly, though by stronger men eventually subdued. " Coldness and want of passion in a picture are not signs of its accuracy, but of the paucity of its statements." [4] " Pour faire de bons vers, il faut avoir le diable au corps," said Voltaire. Macaulay had far too little of the "diable au corps" to make him a writer of impressive individuality and real power. The extent of his fame is out of all proportion to its depth. Except a certain influence on the style of journalism, which threatens to be transient, he has left little mark on his age. Out of his millions of readers there has scarcely come one genuine disciple.

By a change of taste as remarkable as any in literature, his style, which was universally admired, is now very freely decried—perhaps more than justice requires. It cannot be denied that it was a new style : all contemporaries, headed by Jeffrey, agreed upon that point. Real novelty of style is generally a safe test of originality of mind and character. With Macaulay the test does not extend so far. Still his style is perhaps the most original thing about him. Its peculiarity is the skill with which he has imparted to written language a large portion of the swing and rush of spoken oratory. He can be read with a good deal of the pleasurable excitement which numbers of people feel in listening to facile and voluble discourse. As a rule, copious and fluent oratory makes very bad reading : but Macaulay had the secret of transposing his thoughts from the language of spoken discourse, which seems their proper vehicle, to the language of written prose, without loss of effect. To no one talent

[4] *Modern Painters,* vol. i.

perhaps does he owe so much of his reputation. The
more refined and delicate literary styles are unpopular in
proportion to their excellence ; their harmonies and intervals, fascinating to the cultivated ear, are not only lost on
but somewhat offensive to the multitude. For one hearer
thrilled by a sonata or a fugue, a thousand are delighted
by what are sometimes called the spirit-stirring strains
of *Rule Britannia*. At an early date Macaulay gauged
the popular taste. In 1830 he wrote to Macvey Napier
complaining that some of the " most pointed and orna-
mented sentences " in an article had been omitted. " Probably," he continues, " in estimating the real value of
any tinsel which I may put upon my articles, you and I
should not materially differ. But it is not by his own
taste, but by the taste of the fish, that the angler is determined in his choice of bait." It would be unfair to dwell
on such a remark in a private letter, if it stood alone.
But all his practice during thirty years was in unison
with the principle here laid down. Eschewing high
thought on the one hand, and deep feeling on the other,
he marched down a middle road of resonant commonplace,
quite certain that where

> Bang, whang, whang, goes the drum,
> And tootle-tee-tootle the fife,

the densest crowd, marching in time, will follow the music.
Still it is the air rather than the instrument which makes
some persons inclined to stop their ears. It is quite true
that the measures of Macaulay's prose " are emphatically
the measures of spoken deliverance ; " but the spoken
deliverance is of the bar, the hustings, or the House of
Commons. The want of benignity, the hard and scolding
precision, with which he has been justly reproached, are

due rather to the matter and substance than to the form
of his speech. His tone of sentiment is such as would lose
nothing by being uttered in a loud voice at a public
meeting, and he is indeed far from reaching the highest
notes of solemn elevation and simple pathos with which
such an audience inspires some orators. But neither in
public nor in private had Macaulay any gift for expressing
either tender or lofty emotion. His letters are singularly
wanting in effusion and expansiveness, even when
addressed to friends and relatives for whom we know he
had warm affection ! But his love took the form of solid
matter-of-fact kindness, not of a sympathy in delicate
unison with another spirit with whom an interchange of
sentiment is a need of existence. He seems to have been
one of those thoroughly good-hearted good-natured persons
who are wanting in tact, delicacy, and sensitiveness.[5] A
certain coarseness of fibre is unmistakable. Nothing else

[5] He was benevolent, but unsympathetic ; he cared not for the
beauty of nature, he detested dogs, and, except a narrow group of
relations and friends, he cared not for men. One of the least
pleasant passages in his biography is a scene he had with an
Italian custom-house officer, who asked to be allowed a seat in his
carriage from Velletri to Mola ; Macaulay refused. Of this there is
nothing to be said ; the man may easily have been an undesirable
companion. But the comment on the incident is wanting in the
right tone: "I gave him three crowns not to plague by searching my
baggage. . . . He pocketed the three crowns, but looked very dark
and sullen at my refusal to accept his company. Precious fellow !
to think that a public functionary to whom a little silver is a bribe,
is fit company for an English gentleman." Narrow and unintelligent. In mere knowledge, Macaulay could certainly have derived
much more from the man than the latter from Macaulay. But he
had little curiosity or interest in the minds of others. It will be remembered in what isolation he spent his time on the voyage to India.
"Except at meals, I hardly exchanged a word with any human
being." One cannot imagine Socrates or Johnson acting thus.

will account for the "mean and ignoble association" of
ideas, which he often seems rather to seek than avoid.
He prefers comparisons which, by their ungraduated,
unsoftened abruptness, produce a shock on nerves less
robust than his own. "The victuallers soon found out
with whom they had to deal, and sent down to the fleet
casks of meat which dogs would not touch, and barrels of
beer which smelt worse than bilge water." Nothing is
gained by such crudity of language ; and truth is sacrificed,
if that is a consideration. Dogs have no objection to
tainted meat, and nothing can smell worse than bilge
water. "For our part, if we are forced to make our
choice between the first shoemaker and the author of the
three books on Anger, we pronounce for the shoemaker;"
and one may add, you are certain to gain the gallery's
applause by so doing. "To the seared consciences of
Shaftesbury and Buckingham the death of an innocent
man gave no more uneasiness than the death of a par-
tridge." "A husband would be justly derided who
should bear from a wife of exalted rank and spotless
virtue, half the insolence which the King of England bore
from concubines who, while they owed everything to his
bounty, caressed his courtiers almost before his face."
Sentences like these, in which the needless emphasis of
the words shows up the more plainly the deficient dignity
and weight of thought, are of frequent occurrence, and
deprive Macaulay's prose of the high quality of distinction.
His comparison of Montesquieu with the learned pig and
musical infant is in the same style. But perhaps the
most striking instance of his tendency to a low-pitched
strain of allusion is to be found in his journal, on the
occasion of his visit to Dumbarton Castle in the last year
of his life: "I remember my first visit to Dumbarton,

and the old minister who insisted on our eating a bit of
cake with him, and said a grace over it which might have
been prologue to a dinner at the Fishmongers' Company
or the Grocers' Company." The notion that the size and
sumptuousness of a feast are to determine the length and
fervour of the thanksgiving, is one which one hardly
expects to find outside of the Common Council, if even it
is to be met with there. Macaulay's utter inability to
comprehend piety of mind, is one of the most singular
traits in his character, considering his antecedents.

Macaulay's style, apart from its content, presents one
or two interesting problems which one would like to
solve. An able critic has noticed the singular fact,
that though he seems to take pains to be pleonastic and
redundant, he is nevertheless invariably lively.[6] His
variations of one tune do not weary, as one might expect.
In the same way, the oratorical swing and rapidity which
he undoubtedly possesses do not appear easy to reconcile
with his short sentences and the mechanically regular
stroke of his periods. His paragraphs are often built up
by a succession of tiers, one over the other ; they do not
seem to grow from a central root of thought or sentiment.
Sentences not exceeding a line in average length, reduced
to their lowest terms of subject, predicate, and copula, are
held together only by the art of the typographer. "The
people of Gloucester rose, and delivered Lovelace from confinement. An irregular army soon gathered around him.
Some of his horsemen had only halters for bridles. Many
of his infantry had only clubs for weapons." The
monotony of rhythm is sometimes reinforced by the
monotony of phrase, sentence after sentence beginning

---

[6] *Hours in a Library*, by L. Stephen, 3rd series.

with the same words; as, for instance, this conclusion of the *Essay on Lord Holland.*

The time is coming when, perhaps, a few old men, the last survivors of our generation, will in vain seek, amidst new streets, and squares, and railway stations, for the sight of that dwelling which was in their youth the favourite resort of wits and beauties—of painters and poets—of scholars, philosophers, and statesmen. *They will then remember,* with strange tenderness, many objects once familiar to them—the avenue and the terrace, the busts and the paintings; the carving, the grotesque gilding, and the enigmatic mottoes. With peculiar fondness *they will recall* that venerable chamber, in which all the antique gravity of a college library was so singularly blended with all that female grace and wit could devise to embellish a drawing-room. *They will recollect,* not unmoved, those shelves loaded with the varied learning of many lands and many ages; those portraits in which were preserved the features of the best and wisest Englishmen of two generations. *They will recollect* how many men who have guided the politics of Europe—who have moved great assemblies by reason and eloquence—who have put life into bronze and canvas, or who have left to posterity things so written as it shall not willingly let them die—were there mixed with all that was loveliest and gayest in the society of the most splendid of capitals. *They will remember* the singular character which belonged to that circle in which every talent and accomplishment, every art and science, had its place. *They will remember* how the last debate was discussed in one corner, and the last comedy of Scribe in another; while Wilkie gazed with modest admiration on Reynolds's Baretti; while Mackintosh turned over Thomas Aquinas to verify a quotation; while Talleyrand related his conversations with Barras at the Luxemburg, or his rides with Lannes over the field of Austerlitz. *They will remember,* above all, the grace—and the kindness, far more admirable than grace—with which the princely hospitality of that ancient mansion was dispensed. *They will remember* the venerable and benignant countenance and the cordial voice of him who bade them welcome. *They will remember* that temper which years of pain, of sickness, of lameness, of confinement, seemed only to make sweeter and sweeter ; and that frank politeness, which at once relieved all the embarrassment of the youngest and most timid writer or artist who found himself for the first time among ambassadors and earls. *They will remember* that constant flow of conversation, so natural, so animated, so various, so rich with observation and anecdote ; that wit which never gave a wound ; that exquisite mimicry which ennobled, instead of degrading, that goodness of heart which appeared in every look and accent, and gave additional value to every talent and acquirement. *They will remember,* too, that he whose name they hold in reverence was not less distinguished by the inflexible uprightness of his political conduct than by his loving disposition and winning manners. *They will remember* that in the last lines which he traced he expressed his joy that he had done nothing unworthy of the friend of Fox and Grey ; and they will have reason to feel similar joy, if, in looking back on many troubled years, they cannot accuse themselves of having done anything unworthy of men who were distinguished by the friendship of Lord Holland.

If the light of nature and an ordinary ear were not sufficient to warn a writer against such repetition, Macaulay, who had read his Aristotle and Quinctilian, might have been expected to know better. " The qualities and artifices of style which tell in declamation, for which they were intended, when divested of this aid do not fulfil their proper function ; as, for instance, asyndeta and the reiteration of the same word ; and though the orators employ them in their debates, as adapted to delivery, *in the written style they appear silly, and are justly re-probated.*" [7] Indeed, Macaulay never quite overcame a

[7] Cope's *Introduction to Aristotle's Rhetoric,* p. 326.

tendency to abuse this common and useful rhetorical figure in an order of composition for which it is unfit. It is to be found in the first page of his *History*, and is so common in his *Essays*, that their style is very often identical with that of his speeches.

The art by which Macaulay has caused these various blemishes not only to be condoned, but to be entirely unperceived by the majority of readers, is derived from the imaginative power and splendour of his larger tableaux. The sentences may be aggregates of atoms, but the whole is confluent, and marked by masterly unity. Style may be considered from more than one aspect. We may consider it from the point of view of the grammarian or professor of rhetoric, with reference mainly to the choice of words, the propriety of phrase, the rhythm of sentence. Or we may consider it from the higher standpoint—the general effect and impressiveness of the whole composition; the pervading power, lucidity, and coherence, which make a book attractive to read and easy to master. In the former class of qualities Macaulay leaves much to be desired. In the latter he has not many superiors. Artless, and almost clumsy as he is in building a sentence, into which he is without the skill to weave, as some moderns do,

Those lesser thirds so plaintive, sixths diminished sigh on sigh,—

in building a chapter, an article, or a book he has a grand and easy power which ought "to bring the sweat into the brow" of some who hold him cheap. His short sentences, when looked at by themselves so isolated and thin, are the lines of a fine engraving all converging to produce one well-considered artistic effect—an effect in which neither deep thought nor high feeling has a share, but still one so brilliant and striking that the criticism which overlooks it may justly be accused of blindness.

CHAPTER III.

WE sometimes hear Macaulay's Essays preferred to his
History, not only as more popular, but as showing more
genius and power. Although this opinion could hardly
be held by any serious critic, it contains enough truth to
make its existence intelligible. The Essays have qualities
of variety, freedom, and, above all, brevity, which the
History is necessarily without, but which are very taking
qualities with the readers whom Macaulay chiefly ad-
dresses. A long-sustained work devoted to the history
of one country in one period, however lively it may be
made, demands a heavier tax on the attention than many
are able to pay. The large and ever-growing class who
read not for knowledge but for amusement, as an innocent mode of killing time, soon become weary of
one subject carried on through several volumes. Their
weak mental appetite needs stimulating by a frequent
change of diet. Length is the one thing they fear and
most dislike. To take up the same work day after day
oppresses them with the sense of a task, and they
promptly conceive an ill-will to the author for not keep-
ing pace with their changes of mood. Even the highest
works of poetical genius—the *Faery Queen* and *Paradise
Lost*—are said to be comparatively neglected, simply on

account of their volume, which alarms the indolence of readers. And it may be well doubted whether even Shakespeare does not owe a great deal of his popularity with the reading public to the fact that plays are necessarily short, and can be read through in a short time.

To readers of this temper—and they probably are a vast majority—essays offer the very thing they are in search of. No strain on the attention, frequent change of subject, a happy medium between undue length and undue brevity, are qualities exactly suited to their taste. This alone might well be the sole or chief reason why Macaulay's Essays should be by some preferred to his History. But this is probably not the only reason. The Essays *have* some merits which the History lacks. They were all written in the vigour of life, before his mind was saddened, if not enfeebled, by serious ill-health. They were short enough to be struck off at a heat, and many we know were written with extreme rapidity. They consequently have the attractive quality of exuberant vigour, high spirits, and conscious strength which delights in exercise and rapid motion for their own sake. A sense of weariness in the writer, however much it may be concealed by art, is almost sure to be felt by the reader sympathetically. Of this drawback few authors ever knew less than Macaulay up to the time of his illness. His prompt and full command of his faculties made, as he said, composition nothing but a pleasure to him. No man ever worshipped a more bountiful muse. He had no labour pains, no dark wrestlings with thoughts which he could not throw, conquered and subdued, with vigorous strength down on paper. His Essays therefore, in many ways much less finished and careful, have often more *verve* than the History. Like the first flight of the

F 2

falcon, they show a store of unsubdued energy, which, so far from fearing fatigue, rather seeks it, and does not readily find it.

The originality of form and treatment which Macaulay gave to the historical essay has not perhaps received due recognition. Without having invented it, he so greatly expanded and improved it that he deserves nearly as much credit as if he had. He did for the historical essay what Haydn did for the sonata, and Watt for the steam engine : he found it rudimentary and unimportant, and left it complete and a thing of power. Before his time, there was the ponderous history—generally in quarto— and there was the antiquarian dissertation. There was also the historical review, containing alternate pages of extract and comment—generally rather dull and gritty. But the historical essay as he conceived it, and with the prompt inspiration of a real discoverer immediately put into practical shape, was as good as unknown before him. To take a bright period or personage of history, to frame it in a firm outline, to conceive it at once in article-size, and then to fill in this limited canvas with sparkling anecdote, telling bits of colour, and facts all fused together by a real genius for narrative, was the sort of genre-painting which Macaulay applied to history. We have only to turn to the back numbers of the *Edinburgh Review* to perceive how his articles gleam in those old pages of "grey paper and blunt type." And to this day his Essays remain the best of their class, not only in England but in Europe. Slight, or even trivial, in the field of historical erudition and critical inquiry, they are masterpieces if regarded in the light of great popular cartoons on subjects taken from modern history. They are painted indeed with such freedom, vividness, and power, that they may be said to enjoy a sort of tacit monopoly of the periods and characters to which they refer, in the estimation of the general public. How many persons, outside the class of professed students, know much of Lord Chatham, Lord Clive, Warren Hastings, Walpole, Pulteney, Carteret, and many more, beyond what they learn from the pages of Macaulay? His friend Lord Stanhope is a much more safe, steady, and trustworthy guide through the eighteenth century. But for one reader who will sit down to the accurate, conscientious, ill-written *History of England* by Lord Stanhope, a hundred will read, and read again, the brilliant Essays. Any portion of English history which Macaulay has travelled over—the remark applies much less to his treatment of foreign subjects—is found to be moulded into a form which the average Englishman at once enjoys and understands. He did, it has been truly said, in a small way, and in solid prose, the same thing for the seventeenth and eighteenth centuries that Shakespeare did in a poetical way for the fifteenth century. The first Duke of Marlborough had the candour to acknowledge that all he knew of the history of England he derived from Shakespeare's historical plays. We may surmise, that many who would not readily confess it are equally indebted to Macaulay. He succeeded in achieving the object which he always professed to aim at—making history attractive and interesting—to a degree never attained before. This is either a merit or a fault, according to the point of view from which we regard it; but from every point of view it was no common feat.

It will be convenient to classify the Essays in the following groups, with the object of giving as much unity as possible to a subject necessarily wanting it :—

(1.) English history.

(2.) Foreign history.

(3.) Controversial.

(4.) Critical and miscellaneous.

(1.) *English History Group.*[1]—If the articles composing this group are arranged with reference to the chronology of the periods they treat of, they form a fairly complete survey of English history from the time of Elizabeth to the later years of the reign of George III. This was the portion of our history to which Macaulay had devoted most time and attention. The period previous to the Reformation he had studied with much less care. His acquaintance with the Middle Age generally, may without injustice be pronounced slight ; and though well informed as to the history of the Continent, his knowledge of it, as we shall have occasion to see, was not so accurate or deep. But his knowledge of English history in the seventeenth and eighteenth centuries was minute, extensive, and profound. These twelve essays may be regarded as preliminary studies, by which he preluded and prepared himself for his great work. Nothing can be more obvious than that the historical student was guided in his choice of this field by the sympathies and opinions of the active politician. He was a Whig, with ardent and disinterested conviction, when to be a Whig was to be a friend of liberty and progress in the most rational and practical form. During the long predominance of Tory rule and sentiment, the heroic age of England had been defaced, and perverted into a hideous and malignant caricature. A vigorous vindication of English liberty in the past, allied itself naturally, in the pages of the *Edinburgh*

[1] Burleigh, Hallam, Hampden, Milton Temple, Mackintosh, Walpole, Pitt-Chatham, Clive, Warren Hastings.

Review, with the active polemics there carried on in favour of the same liberty in the present. It was not as an antiquarian that Macaulay insisted upon a new hearing of the great cause in which Charles I., Strafford, and Laud appeared on the one side, against Hampden, Pym, and Cromwell on the other; but as the active member of Parliament, who supported the first Reform Bill with five powerful speeches in one year. He attacked Toryism indirectly, by writing on the great Liberal leaders of the seventeenth and eighteenth centuries, as the Reformers attacked Catholicism by writing on the primitive discipline and doctrine of the Early Church. When writing of the Long Parliament or the Revolution, an implied reference is always visible to the Whigs and Tories of his own day. Sometimes the reference to contemporary politics is open and direct, as when, in the midst of his discussion of the conduct of the Parliamentary leaders headed by Hampden, he makes a sudden and telling allusion to the contemporary condition of Spain under Ferdinand VII. (Memorials of Hampden).

The party character of Macaulay's Essays on English History is neither to be denied nor deplored. That he rendered a great political service to the cause of Liberalism cannot be doubted, and every deduction that may be made from the merit of the historian must be set down to the account of the publicist. Scientific history was never his object, but the propagation of sound constitutional doctrine was very much so. It has been said with truth, that in all he ever wrote, a defence open or implied of Whig principles may be perceived. That this connexion of his work with the ephemeral politics of the day will injure its permanent value is very obvious; but not perhaps to the extent that is sometimes supposed.

It is one of the affectations of the hour to use the term Whig as a convenient vehicle of polite vituperation. A man now who can with any accuracy be called a genuine old Whig, is by some persons considered to be beyond the pale of toleration. No further anathema is needed; the deadliest slur has been cast on his intellect and character in one word. A hatred of pure reason, and a comfortable middle-class creed on social matters, are the two most offensive characteristics generally ascribed to the Whig. They would be offensive enough, if Whiggism was, or pretended to be, a philosophical theory of politics. But in Macaulay's day, Whiggism was not a philosophy, but a scheme of practical expediency—a working policy which had a chance of being realized. What after all is the essence of Whiggism as distinct from its accidents? Is it not this—illogical but practical compromise, between two extremes which are logical but not at all practical? It is no isolated phenomenon confined to certain periods of English history, but one of the most general to be found, not only in politics but in religion, and even philosophy. Wherever men are engaged in steering between the opposite shoals of extreme parties with a view to practical results, there Whiggism exists in reality if not in name. Bossuet was a Whig in the Catholic Church, and Pascal was a Whig in the Gallican Church. Reid, Brown, and Coleridge, even Kant, were Whigs in philosophy. Whiggism is always the scorn of thoroughgoing men and rigorous logicians; is ever stigmatized as a bending of the knee to Baal. But thoroughgoing men, actuated by thoroughgoing logic, do not often, or for long, remain directors of public affairs. No man was ever less of a philosopher, or more of a politician, than Macaulay. He had an eye to business, not to abstract truth. The present age, which

sees only the writer, and has nearly forgotten the politician, is easily tempted to judge him by a standard to
which he did not and could not conform.   His own
serene unconsciousness of his want of speculative power is
at once amusing and irritating.   But the point to be
remembered is, that when we have written Whig after
his name, and declared they are convertible terms, all is
not said and done, and that for purposes of criticism,
the process is too simple and summary to be of much
value.   We have to consider the object at which he
aimed, not to complain of his failure to hit a mark which
he never thought of.   A man engaged in paving the best
via media that he can find between ultra opinions on opposite sides, is always exposed to taunt.   Macaulay was reviled by Chartists and Churchmen, and he himself disliked
high Tories and philosophical Radicals in equal measure.
When the object is to gain votes for practical measures,
the beauties of pure reason are apt to be overlooked.
The great maxim of prudence on these occasions, is "not
to go too far" in any direction.   Logic and consistency
are readily sacrificed for the sake of union in action.
Closet philosophers naturally resent this as very mean
and commonplace.   But that is because they are closet
philosophers.

The party bias of the Essays, it is said, deprives them
of all value as history.   And this is partly true.
But let us be just even to party historians.   When
it is claimed that the historian must above all things
be impartial, what is meant by the word?   Is it
demanded that the writer on a past age is to take no
side—to have no preference, either for persons whom
he considers virtuous or for principles which he considers
just; and, again, is he to have no reprobation for the

contraries to these, which he considers unjust and pernicious? If this is meant by impartiality, the answer is that on these lines history cannot be, and never has been, written. Such is the solidarity of human nature, that it refuses to regard the just and the unjust with equal favour in the past any more than in the present. Of course the question is always reserved as to which party in the suit these epithets respectively apply. Erroneous judgments have been passed in the court of history, as they are passed in courts of law. But that is no argument for maintaining that both sides are entitled to the same favour and good will. Both sides are entitled to justice, and justice may require the utmost severity of condemnation of one of the parties. No judge at the end of a criminal trial was ever able to conceal the side to which he inclined in his summing up. His business is not to abstain from having an opinion, which a man of intelligence could hardly do, but to point to the decisive evidence on either side, and holding up the scales, to let the lighter kick the beam in the eyes of all men. If this is partiality, it is such as no honest man would like to be without. So the historian; his duty is to be impartial in weighing evidence; but that being done, to declare with unmistakable clearness which side has been found wanting. As he is human, he is exposed to error, but for that there is no remedy. Miscarriages of justice must and will occur. They must be redressed when discovered. And fortunately errors of this kind are of less grave practical consequence in the courts of history than in the courts of law. Yet we submit to the latter, being unable to help ourselves. It is vain to hope that this subjective bias can ever be removed from the mind of a human judge. And it is not desirable to

remove it.   What is worthy of blame is the suppression
or garbling of evidence—not holding really true scales.
The notion that such bias is necessarily connected with
the party-spirit of modern times, and shown only in
reference to modern periods of history, is quite without
foundation.   The history of Greece and Rome is subject
to it as much as the history of Modern Europe.   Mitford
was biassed in favour of the oligarchies of Greece.   Grote
was equally biassed in favour of the democracies.   So far
each was within his right.   But if it appears that
either was unfair in collecting and sifting evidence, and
showed anxiety to win a verdict by his mispresentation of
it, then he is to be condemned as an unjust judge—or
rather, he is an advocate, who has usurped a judge's
functions and merits degradation.   Mitford has been
deposed, and justly so, in the opinion of competent men.
Grote on the whole has been maintained by the same
opinion.

Further, if we grant that historians are exposed to
peculiar temptations to slide from the position of judge to
that of advocate—if they are honest advocates, maintaining
the cause they believe to be just, by honourable means,
they need not fear much censure from equitable men.
The final judge, after all, is public opinion—not of a day,
or a year, or even of a century, but of ages.   Perhaps it
can never be absolutely obtained.   But in the meanwhile
nothing is more serviceable to the cause of truth than that
every important party to an historical suit should be
represented by the ablest advocate that can be found, so
long as he is honest—that is, not only refrains from telling lies, but from suppressing truth.   Every open-minded
inquirer must be glad to hear all that can be said in
favour of a given side ; nay, to hear most of all what

can be said in favour of the side to which he himself does
not belong.   It is vastly more comforting to hear Dr
Lingard condemn James II. of injustice, infatuation,
arbitrary and impotent policy, than to hear the most
eloquent indictments of the same monarch from those who
hold Whig opinions.   When Hume condemns Charles I.
for the arrest of the five members, we feel quite sure that
on that point at least nothing can be said, or such an
able, not to say unscrupulous, advocate, would not have
omitted it.   In time the heats of party zeal are gradually
cooled ; questions of disputed fact are reduced to narrow
issues.   The motives and characters of the most prominent
actors are at last weighed by impartial men, who have no
interest stronger in the matter than the discovery of
truth.   Then we have reached the critical stage of
history.

Macaulay was far from having reached this higher
stage.   But as a writer of party history he stands
high.   If his mind was uncritical, his temper was
generally fair.   No one would expect the party against
whom he appeared—the sympathizers with high preroga-
tive, as against the sympathizers with liberty,—to admit
this.   But his Whig version of our history has been on
the whole accepted by a wide public, with whom political
partisanship is not a strong passion.   His frank avowal of
his sympathies can be a defect only in the eyes of the
unintelligent, or the bigoted who will brook no contradiction.   His bias is open and above-board ; he lays his
proofs before you, which you may accept or refuse ; but
in a candid way—very different from the sly, subtle
disingenuousness of Hume.   At the same time it must be
admitted that the common fate of controversialists is
already beginning to overtake Macaulay.   His point of

view is already somewhat out of date. We are always
repelled, or disdainfully amused, by the heats of a remote
controversy which does not touch our passions or interests.
It seems absurd to be so angry with people who lived so
long ago, and who clearly never did us any harm. The
suave mari magno feeling is a little ungenerous, but
very natural and common. A critic complains that
Macaulay "mauls poor James II." as he did the Tories
of 1832. It no doubt requires an historical imagination
of some liveliness to make us perceive that pity is wasted
on a sovereign whose wickedness was only defeated by
his folly. We are in no danger of being tried and brow-
beaten by Jeffreys or hanged by Colonel Kirke. Such are
the gratitude and the "little short memories" of mankind.
Nevertheless it is a true instinct which warns us against
transferring the passions of the present to the remote past.
The passions should be quiet, only the critical reason
should be active, surveying the concluded story with calm
width, and telling us what it all amounted to.

It will not be expected that all Macaulay's Essays
should be passed in review in a short work of this kind.
We can only find space for a few words on the most
memorable, omitting the less famous as we pass over the
relatively unimportant pictures in a gallery.

The Essays, as might well be supposed, are unequal in
merit. One of the weakest is that which appears first on
the list given a few pages back, *Burleigh and his Times.*
It is at once thin and trenchant, and would be wholly un-
deserving of notice did it not contain a faulty historical
view, which Macaulay never laid aside to the end of his life.
The error consists in fastening the odium of persecution
and intolerance as a peculiar reproach on the government of Burleigh and Elizabeth. "What can be said in

defence of a ruler who is at once indifferent and intolerant ?" he asks.   If the Queen had only had the virtue and enlightenment of More and L'Hospital, the whole of our history for the last two hundred and fifty years would have worn another colour.   " She had the happiest opportunity ever vouchsafed to any sovereign of establishing perfect freedom of conscience throughout her dominions, without danger to her Government, without scandal to any large party among her subjects."   Any addition to the enlightenment and patience of the capricious vixen who then ruled England would no doubt have been a great boon to her subjects and ministers, but it is supposing extraordinary efficacy even in the virtue of Queen Elizabeth to imagine that it could have influenced our history for two hundred and fifty years after her death. But Macaulay must have known that uniformity in religion was considered in the sixteenth century an indispensable condition of stable civil government, and that by all parties and sects.   " Persecution for religious heterodoxy in all its degrees was in the sixteenth century the principle, as well as the practice, of every church.   It was held inconsistent with the sovereignty of the magistrate to permit any religion but his own ; inconsistent with his duty to suffer any but the true." [2]   Bacon said : " It is certain that heresies and schisms are of all others the greatest scandals, yea, more than corruption of manners." [3]   It is against all equity to blame one or two individuals for a universal error.   Yet Macaulay constantly dwells on the persecutions of Elizabeth's reign as if they were marked by peculiar shortsightedness and malignity.   He does it in the essay on *Hallam*, and in the first chapter of the

[2] Hallam's *Literature of Europe*, vol. ii. p. 343.
[3] Essay iii.

History, though in less peremptory language. There can be no doubt that he knew the facts perfectly well. But, as often happened with him, knowledge did not mount up into luminous general views. Persecution had long been proved to be bad; Elizabeth persecuted; therefore she was to be blamed. The temper of the whole age is not taken into the account.

The article on *Hallam's Constitutional History* is one of the best. It is one of the most strenuous argumentative pieces Macaulay ever wrote. Fiercely polemical in its assault on the Tory version of English history, it may be regarded as a compendium of Whig principles *in usum populi*. Indeed its opinions are somewhat more than Whig. It belongs to that small group of articles which were written before the author was plunged in the daily strife of politics and ceaseless round of business, (the others are those on *Milton*, *Machiavelli*, and *History*,) and they show, I venture to think, a speculative reach and openness of mind which were never recovered in the active life of subsequent years. The vindication of the character of Cromwell is as spirited as it is just, and really gives the outline which Carlyle filled in many years after.

The article on the *Memorials of Hampden* is graceful and touching. The tone of pious reverence for the great Puritan champion makes it one of his most harmonious pieces. The essay on *Milton* is only remarkable for showing the early maturity of his powers, but on that ground it is very remarkable. With the article on *Sir William Temple* we enter upon a new stage of Macaulay's development as a writer and an artist. The articles he wrote for the *Edinburgh Review* after his return from India in 1838, are markedly superior to those he wrote before leaving England. The tone is much quieter, yet the vivacity is not diminished; the composition is more careful, sustained, and even. The *Sir William Temple* was the first of the post-Indian articles, and it is one of the best he ever wrote. If one wanted to give an intelligent foreign critic a good specimen of Macaulay—a specimen in which most of his merits and fewest of his faults are collected in a small compass—one could hardly do better than give him the article on *Sir William Temple*. The extraordinary variety of the piece, the fine colouring and judicious shading, the vivid interest, the weighty topics discussed gravely, the lighter accessories thrown in gracefully over and around the main theme, like arabesque work on a Moorish mosque, or flights of octaves and arpeggios in a sonata of Mozart, justly entitle it to a high place, not only in Macaulay's writings, but in the literature of the age. Strange to say, it does not appear to have been a favourite with the public, if we may infer as much from the fact that it has not been printed separately; yet no article deserves it better. It is a masterpiece of its kind. The article on *Mackintosh* calls for no remark. That on *Walpole* is interesting chiefly for the amusing animosity which Macaulay nourished towards him. It was most unjust. He had far too low an opinion of Walpole's intellect, which was in many ways more penetrating and thoughtful than his own. Walpole did not call Montesquieu a Parisian coxcomb, but the very moment the *Esprit des Lois* appeared, pronounced it the best book that ever was written. Walpole's generous sentiments on the slave-trade, half a century in advance of public opinion on the subject, should have been appreciated by a son of Zachary Macaulay. The two articles on the first William Pitt, written at ten years' interval, show the difference between Macaulay's earlier and later manner very clearly. The first is full of dash, vigour, and interest, but in a somewhat boisterous tone of high spirits, which at times runs dangerously near to bad taste. As for instance :—

"In this perplexity Newcastle sent for Pitt, hugged him, patted him, smirked at him, wept over him, and lisped out the highest compliments and the most splendid promises. The king, who had hitherto been as sulky as possible, would be civil to him at the *levée*," &c., &c. Nothing of this kind will be found in the second article (the last Macaulay ever wrote for the *Edinburgh Review*), but, on the contrary, great dignity and gravity which recall the best pages of the *History*. He was, indeed, writing the *History* at this moment, and he was enjoying a literary leisure such as he had never enjoyed before. He also was losing the strongly marked characteristics of a party man, and gravitating to that central and neutral position which he occupied with regard to politics in his later years. The fact is worth alluding to, as there seems still to survive a notion that Macaulay from first to last remained a narrow and bitter Whig. Those who hold this view may consider the following passage :—

The Whig, who during three Parliaments had never given one vote against the Court, and who was ready to sell his soul for the Comptroller's staff or for the Great Wardrobe, still professed to draw his political doctrines from Locke and Milton, still worshipped the memory of Pym and Hampden, and would still, on the 30th of January, take his glass to the man in the mask and then to the man who would do it without a mask. The Tory, on the other hand, while he reviled the mild and temperate Walpole as a deadly enemy of liberty, could see nothing to reprobate in the iron tyranny of Strafford and Laud. But whatever judgment the Whig or the

Tory of that age might pronounce on transactions long past, there can be no doubt that, as respected practical questions then pending, the Tory was a reformer—and indeed an intemperate and indiscreet reformer—while the Whig was a conservative, even to bigotry. . . . . Thus the successors of the old Cavaliers had turned demagogues ; the successors of the old Roundheads had turned courtiers. Yet it was long before their mutual animosity began to abate; for it is the nature of parties to retain their original enmities far more firmly than their original principles. During many years a generation of Whigs whom Sydney would have spurned as slaves, continued to wage deadly war with a generation of Tories whom Jeffreys would have hanged for republicans.

The Pitts, both father and son, seem to have had an unusual attraction for Macaulay, and he wrote of them with more sympathy and insight than of any other statesman except King William III. His biography of the younger Pitt is perhaps the most perfect thing that he has left. It is not an historical essay, but a genuine " Life," and it is impossible to overpraise either the plan or the execution. Nearly all the early faults of his rhetorical manner have disappeared ; there is no eloquence, no declamation, but a lofty moral impressiveness which is very touching and noble. It was written when he saw his own death to be near, and although he had none of Johnson's " horror of the last," there is a depth and solemnity of tone in this " Life " to which he never attained before. Pitt's own stately and majestic character would seem to have chastened and elevated his style, which recalls the masculine dignity, gravity, and calm peculiar to the higher strains of Roman eloquence. The little work deserves printing by itself on " papier de Chine," in Elzevir type, by Lemerre, Quantin, or the Librairie des Bibliophiles.

Very different are the two famous Indian articles on
Clive and Warren Hastings.   In these we find no Attic
severity of diction, but all the pomp and splendour of
Asiatic eloquence.   It is not unsuitable to the occasion ;
a somewhat gorgeous magnificence is not out of place
in the East.   There is no need to dwell on pieces so
universally and justly popular.[4]   They belong, it need not
be said to his second and better manner ; the rhetoric
though proud and high-stepping enough, is visibly under
restraint and amenable to the curb.   There was a particular reason why Macaulay was so successful in the articles
on the two Pitts and the two Indian Pro-consuls.   They
were men whose character he could thoroughly understand and largely admire.   Taken all round, his insight
into men's bosoms was not deep, and was decidedly
limited.   Complex and involved characters, in which the
good and evil were interwoven in odd and original ways,
in which vulgar and obvious faults or vices concealed
deeper and rarer qualities underneath, were beyond his
ken.   In men like Rousseau, Byron, Boswell, even Walpole, he saw little more than all the world could see —
those patent breaches of conventional decorum and morality

[4] It is vexatious to be forced to add, that the historical fidelity
of the fine *Essay on Warrren Hastings*, is in many places open to
more than suspicion.   A son of the Chief Justice of Bengal has
shown (*Memoirs of Sir Elijah Impey*, Simpkin, Marshall, and Co.,
1840) that Macaulay has been guilty at least of very reckless
statements.   He was not, one likes to think, intentionally and
wittingly unfair ; but he was liable to become inebriated with
his own rhetoric till he lost the power of weighing evidence.   The
old superstitious belief in Macaulay's accuracy is a creed of the
past : but one cannot help regretting that he never saw the propriety or even the necessity of either answering or admitting the
grave reflections on his truthfulness made in Mr. Barwell Impey's
book.

which the most innocent young person could join him in condemning. But the great civic and military qualities—resolute courage, promptitude, self-command and firmness of purpose—he could thoroughly understand and warmly admire. His style is always animated by a warmer glow and a deeper note when he celebrates high deeds of valour or fortitude either in the council or the field. There was an heroic fibre in him, which the peaceful times in which he lived, and the peaceful occupations in which he passed his days, never adequately revealed.

Foreign History Group.[5]—Of these five articles there is only one over which we can linger. The *Machiavelli* is ingenious and wide; but its main thesis—that the Italians had a monopoly of perfidy in the fifteenth and sixteenth centuries, is untenable and almost absurd. The *Mirabeau* is sprightly, but it contains some very commonplace errors—for instance, that the death of the Duke of Burgundy was a serious loss to good government in France. As to the *Frederic*, it might pass muster before Carlyle wrote on the subject: it has little interest now. The article on Barère is a most savage philippic against one of the most odious characters in history. Whether he deserved so sumptuous an execution may be doubted. Alone remains the famous article on the *History of the Popes*, which not only bespeaks attention by reason of its subject and the point of view from which that subject is regarded, but because it is apparently considered by some persons as valuable and important in itself. It is very far indeed from being either. If the articles on Temple and Pitt show Macaulay's good side, this article on the Popes shows his less favourable side in an equal degree. It was not a subject which he was well qualified to treat, even if

[5] Machiavelli, Mirabeau, Von Ranke, Frederic, Barère.

he had done his best and given himself fair play. Circumstances and his own temperament combined, prevented him from doing either one or the other.

The real subject of the article, though nominally Ranke's book, is to ask the question, Why did Protestantism cease to spread after the end of the sixteenth century? and why did the Church of Rome recover so much of the ground that she had lost in the early years of the Reformation? The inquiry was an interesting one, and worthy of a careful answer. But the answer could only be found or given by a student who could investigate with freedom, and who was in a position to speak his mind. To write with one eye on the paper and with the other on the susceptibilities of the religious world, was not a method that could lead to results of any value. And Macaulay comes to no result. He does not even reach a conclusion. The question with which he starts, and which is repeated again with great solemnity at the end of the article, is not answered, nor is an answer even attempted. He displays in his most elaborate manner how strange and surprising it is that the Roman Church should survive the many attacks made upon her; how singular it is that when Papists now forsake their religion, they become infidels and not Protestants; and when they forsake their infidelity, instead of stopping half way in some Protestant faith, they go back to Romanism. At the time of the Reformation, he says, this was not the case. "Whole nations then renounced Popery, without ceasing to believe in a first cause, in a future life, or the Divine Mission of Jesus." This he considers a "most remarkable fact," and worthy of "serious consideration." But he does not give a hint of an explanation of the fact—unless the singular preface to the historical portion of the article may be so considered.

The purpose of this Introduction is to discuss whether
the growth of knowledge and science has any influence in
the way of promoting the rationality of men's religious
opinions ; and Macaulay decides that it has not.   Science
may increase to any amount, but that will never have the
least effect on either natural or revealed religion.

A Christian of the fifth century with a Bible, was neither better
nor worse situated than a Christian of the nineteenth century
with a Bible—candour and natural acuteness being of course
supposed equal.   It matters not at all that the compass, printing, gunpowder, steam, gas, vaccination, and a thousand other
discoveries and inventions, which were unknown in the fifth
century, are familiar to the nineteenth.   None of these discoveries and inventions have the smallest bearing on the question whether man is justified by faith alone, or whether the
invocation of saints is an orthodox practice.   It seems to us,
therefore, that we have no security for the future against the
prevalence of any theological error that has prevailed in time
past among Christian men.

He goes on to say, that when he reflects that a man of
such wisdom and virtue as Sir Thomas More believed in
Transubstantiation, he is unable to see why that doctrine
should not be believed by able and honest men till the
end of time.   No progress of science can make that doctrine more absurd than it is already, or than it ever has
been.   " The absurdity of the literal interpretation *was as
great and as obvious in the sixteenth century as it is now.*"
In fact, the human mind is given up to caprice on these
matters, and obeys no ascertainable law.   " No learning, no
sagacity, affords a security against the greatest errors on
subjects relating to the invisible world."   Whether a man
believes in sense or nonsense with regard to religion is
merely a matter of accident.   But if that is so, what is

there in the least surprising that the Church of Rome has survived so many attacks and perils? why is that fact "most remarkable" and "worthy of serious consideration"? It is expressly stated that reason has nothing to do with these matters. Any old heresy may come to life again at any moment. Any nonsense may be believed by men of learning and sagacity. Then why wonder that one particular form of nonsense is believed? It is a waste of time to marvel at the effects of acknowledged chance. If, indeed, the phenomena recur with considerable regularity and persistence, we may have good reason to suspect a law. In either case Macaulay's procedure was illegitimate. Roman Catholicism is capable of rational explanation, or it is not. If it is, let the inquiry into the moral, social, and intellectual causes of its origin be soberly conducted. If it is not capable of rational explanation, why pronounce its prevalence worthy of consideration and most remarkable?

But what can be said of the passage in which a Christian of the fifth century with a Bible is declared to be neither better nor worse situated than a Christian of the nineteenth century with a Bible? This is to assert that the lapse of time has no effect on the way in which men read, understand, and interpret ancient writings. With regard to any literature such a remark would be most erroneous; but with regard to the Scriptural literature—the Bible—it is erroneous to absurdity. If there is any one thing which varies from age to age more than another, it is the way in which men regard the writings of past generations, whether these be poetry, philosophy, history, or law. But the point of view from which religious writings are regarded is exposed to perturbations of exceptional violence. And yet Macaulay deliberately wrote that the

lapse of fourteen hundred years had, and could have, no
effect on the study of the Scriptures—that a Christian
reading the Bible amid the falling ruins of the
Roman Empire, was in the same position as a Christian
reading the Bible in prosperous England in the reign of
Queen Victoria. A more inept remark was hardly ever
made by a man of education. With regard to what
ancient writings did Macaulay find himself neither better
nor worse situated than a man of the fifth century? Did
he read Plato, as Plotinus or Proclus did? Did he read
Cicero as Macrobius did? or Virgil as Servius did? or
Homer as Eustathius did (a century or two makes no
difference)? Did he even read Pope as Johnson did,
or Congreve, or Cowley, or any writer that ever lived
in an age removed from his own? But the changes
of mental attitude with regard to secular writers are
trivial as compared to the changes which take place with
regard to religious writers. In a similar spirit, he says
that the absurdity of the literal interpretation was as great
and as obvious in the sixteenth century as it is now. This
is tantamount to saying that what appeared obviously
absurd to him was always obviously absurd to everybody.
That the human mind in the course of its development
has gone through great changes in its conceptions of the
universe—of man's position in it—of the order of nature—
seems to have been a notion which he never even remotely
suspected. Did he think that the Pagan Mythology was
as obviously absurd in the time of Homer as it is now?
Did he find the Hindoo Mythology obviously absurd to
religious Brahmins? This is the writing of a man who
cannot by possibility conceive any point of view but his
own.

The remainder of the article is devoted to a description

of what he names the four uprisings of the human intellect
against the Church of Rome. Macaulay painting a picture,
and Macaulay discussing a religious or philosophical question, are two different persons. There is some very attractive and graceful scene-painting in this part of the article.
The Albigensian Crusade is narrated with great spirit,
brevity, and accuracy. What he calls the second rising
up, in the fourteenth century, was not one at all. It was
a quarrel between an ambitious king and an ambitious
pope, in which the latter got the worst of it. His knowledge here is very thin : as when he says that "The
secular authority, long unduly depressed, regained the
ascendant with startling rapidity." What secular authoriy
had been depressed ? There had not been any secular
authority in France from the fall of the Carling Empire till
the gradual establishment of the Capetian Monarchy under
Philip Augustus and his successors. Feudalism had reigned
supreme for three hundred years ; and feudalism in France
was the negation of secular authority, because it was incompatible with any general government. But we cannot
dwell on this point, any more than we can on his treatment of the Reformation, which is full of small slips ; as,
for instance, that "the spirit of Savonarola had nothing
in common with the spirit of religious Protestantism."
Luther, at any rate, did not hold that view, as he re-
published in 1523 Savonarola's *Commentary on the Psalms.*
Again he says that Catholicism was associated in the public
mind of Spain with liberty as well as victory and dominion.
As regards victory and dominion the remark is true ; but
liberty ! The reference is to the period of the Spanish conquest of Mexico by Cortez ; that is so say, to the despotic
reign of Charles V. We have only space to refer to the
odd comparison, or rather contrast, which he draws between

the Church of England and the Church of Rome, the object
of which is to show that the policy of the latter " is the
very masterpiece of human wisdom," whereas the policy of
the Church of England has been very much the reverse.
It takes him three pages to develop his idea, but it all comes
to this, that the Church of Rome knows how to utilize
enthusiasm, and the Church of England does not.   " Place
Ignatius at Oxford : he is certain to become the head of a
formidable secession.   Place John Wesley at Rome : he is
certain to be the first general of a new society devoted to
the interests and honour of the Church."   Now this sentence, and the whole argument of which it is a part, is
very singular, as showing that Macaulay was often not fully
master of the knowledge which we know that he possessed.   When he paints a picture his hand never shakes ;
his imagination for that purpose holds all the facts he
requires in vivid reality before him.   But when he
attempts to generalize, to co-ordinate facts in a general
expression, he breaks down.   As in the present instance ;
the whole history of the Reformation, both in England
and on the Continent, was there to show him that the profound wisdom he ascribed to the Church of Rome existed
only in his own fancy.   Greater caution in handling Luther,
greater prudence with regard to Henry VIII., might, it is
well known, have prevented a schism.   But the case of the
Jansenists was enough to show him how hasty his view
was, if he had given himself time to reflect.   He was well
acquainted with the facts.   In this very article he refers
to the destruction of Port Royal.   But what were the
Jansenists but the Wesleyans of the Church of Rome,
with a singular closeness of analogy ?   He reproaches the
English Church with the defection of Wesley, and no
doubt a great deal may be said as regards the unwisdom

which allowed or caused it.   But what was that compared
to the treatment of the Jansenists by the Church of Rome ?
As a matter of fact, from the time of St. Cyran and
Antony Arnauld to the time of Lammenais and Döllinger,
the Church of Rome has never hesitated to take the
shortest way with dissentients in her own communion,
"to spue them out of her mouth," with every mark of
detestation and abhorrence.   On the other hand, of all
long-suffering Churches, tolerant and docile of contradiction to the verge of feebleness, the Church of England
is perhaps the most remarkable.   And Macaulay knew this
quite well.

Controversial Group.[6]— Controversy is at once the most
popular and the most ephemeral form of composition.
Nothing seems more important at the moment : nothing
less so when the moment has passed.   Of all the endless
controversies of which the world has ever been full, only
the fewest survive in human memory ; and they do so
either because they have been real turning-points in the
history of thought, or because something of permanent
value outside the immediate subject of contention was
struck out in the conflict.   Pascal's *Provincial Letters* are
the supreme example of a controversial piece on which
time seems to have no effect.   But Pascal had advantages
such as no other controversialist has ever united.   First
of all, he did not kill his adversaries, generally the most
fatal thing for his own permanent fame that a controversialist can do.   The Jesuits still exist, and are still
hated by many.   Those who bear ill-will to the Society
find in the *Provincial Letters* the most exquisite expression of their dislike.   Secondly, Pascal was the first

[6] Mill, Saddler, Southey, Gladstone.

classic prose writer of his country. On a lower, but still a very high level, stands Bentley's dissertation on *Phalaris*. Bentley did kill his adversary dead, but it was with missiles of pure gold, which the world carefully preserves. Macaulay, it need hardly be remarked, did nothing of this kind. He took his share with courage and ability in the battle for Liberal views forty and fifty years ago, and that is nearly all that can be said. He kept the position—he repelled the enemy ; he did not advance and occupy new ground, and give a new aspect to the whole campaign. As he suppressed the articles on *Mill*, with a delicacy which did him honour, they need hardly be referred to. It has been well pointed out, that there is a contradiction between his principles and his conduct on this occasion. "He ought by all his intellectual sympathies to be a Utilitarian. Yet he abuses Utilitarianism with the utmost contempt, and has no alternative theory to suggest."[7] But coherence of thought, we have seen, was not his characteristic. The article on *Southey* is much more pleasant reading. If while admiring its vigour we miss a lightness of touch, we should remember that it was written two years before the passing of the Reform Bill, when the minds of men had become heated to a degree of fierceness, The admiration expressed for the industrial *régime* strikes a reader of the present day as oddly sentimental and impassioned. But the industrial *régime* was a very different thing in 1830 from what it is in 1882, and Macaulay was the last man to forecast the future evils of the manufacturing system. As usual, he shows his strength not in thinking, but in drawing. The following passage has always appeared to us as one of the best in his earlier and less chastened manner.

[7] *Hours in a Library*. Third Series. By Leslie Stephen.

Part of this description might, perhaps, apply to a much greater man, Mr. Burke. But Mr. Burke assuredly possessed an understanding admirably fitted for the investigation of truth —an understanding stronger than that of any statesman, active or speculative, of the eighteenth century—stronger than every thing, except his own fierce and ungovernable sensibility. Hence he generally chose his side like a fanatic, and defended it like a philosopher. His conduct, in the most important events of his life—at the time of the impeachment of Hastings, for example, and at the time of the French Revolution—seems to have been prompted by those feelings and motives which Mr. Coleridge has so happily described :

> " Stormy pity, and cherish'd lure
> Of pomp, and proud precipitance of soul."

Hindostan, with its vast cities, its gorgeous pagodas, its long-descended dynasties, its stately etiquette, excited in a mind so capacious, so imaginative, and so susceptible, the most intense interest. The peculiarities of the costume, of the manners, and of the laws, the very mystery which hung over the language and origin of the people, seized his imagination. To plead in Westminster Hall, in the name of the English people, at the bar of the English nobles, for great nations and kings separated from him by half the world, seemed to him the height of human glory. Again, it is not difficult to perceive that his hostility to the French Revolution principally arose from the vexation which he felt at having all his old political associations disturbed, at seeing the well-known boundary-marks of states obliterated, and the names and distinctions with which the history of Europe had been filled for ages, swept away. He felt like an antiquary whose shield had been scoured, or a connoisseur who found his Titian retouched. But however he came by an opinion, he had no sooner got it than he did his best to make out a legitimate title to it. His reason, like a spirit in the service of an enchanter, though spell-bound, was still mighty. It did whatever work his passions and his imagination might impose. But it did that work, however arduous, with marvellous dexterity and vigour. His course was not determined by argument; but he could defend the wildest course by arguments more plausible than those by which common men support opinions which they have adopted, after the fullest deliberation. Reason has scarcely ever displayed, even in those well-constituted minds of which she occupies the throne, so much power and energy as in the lowest offices of that imperial servitude.

The article on Mr. Gladstone's book, *The State in its relations with the Church*, perhaps interests us more than it should, by reason of the courteous but severe handling given to "the young man of unblemished character and distinguished parliamentary talents—the rising hope of those stern and unbending Tories," who have long since looked in another direction for hope and leadership. As regards Macaulay's main contention, that the spiritual and temporal powers should be kept apart as much as possible few now-a-days would dispute it. Mr. Stephen doubts whether we can draw the line between the spiritual and the secular.[8] And in our age of mixed and motley creeds, representing every degree of belief and unbelief, the task may be arduous. The real difficulty is this, that the State always asserts implicitly a creed or doctrine, by its legislation, even when most careful to avoid doing so in an explicit manner. Not to be with a religious doctrine, is to be against it. Even to ignore its claims or existence, is *quoad hoc* to be hostile to them. When the State establishes civil marriage, it puts an affront on the sacrament of marriage ; when it undertakes to teach the commoner elements of morality in its schools, but refuses to further the inculcation of the Christian

[8] *Hours in a Library.* Third Series.

version of those elements, it is so far slighting Christianity.
The result is ceaseless and illogical compromise, extending
over the whole field of politics. And this condition of
things can only be terminated either by the whole population becoming Christian, and identical in creed, or wholly
agnostic. It by no means suited Macaulay's purpose to
say this in the pages of the *Edinburgh Review.* Perhaps
he did not see his way so far. His maxim was—" Remove
always practical grievances. Do not give a thought to
anomalies which are not grievances." Thus he was for
maintaining the Episcopal Church in England, and the
Presbyterian Church in Scotland; and for paying the
Roman Catholic clergy in Ireland. Against these practical
makeshifts there is nothing to be said, if they produce
peace. But in the domain of speculation they have
no place. Mr. Gladstone's position—perhaps not very
logically maintained—was, that the State was bound to be
Christian, after the fashion of the Church of England.
The counter position is, that the State is bound to be
agnostic, after a fashion which nowhere completely exists.
To say this in 1839, would have given rise to unbounded
scandal. Macaulay was so hampered in his argument
that he has been accused " of begging the question by
evading the real difficulty." That may be true enough
from one point of view; but he could hardly have been
expected to write, in that day, very differently from what
he did.

Critical Group.[9]—When Macvey Napier requested
Macaulay to write for him an article on Scott, he made
answer :—" I assure you that I would willingly, and even
eagerly, undertake the subject which you propose, if I

[9] Dryden, R. Montgomery, Byron, Bunyan, Johnson, Bacon,
Hunt, Addison.

thought that I should serve you by doing so. But depend
upon it you do not know what you are asking for . . . . .
I am not successful in analysing the works of genius. I
have written several things on historical, political, and moral
questions, of which, on the fullest re-consideration, I am
not ashamed, and by which I am willing to be estimated :
but I never have written a page of criticism on poetry or
the fine arts which I would not burn if I had the power."
Nothing could be more frank, modest, and true. After
such a candid avowal, it would be ungracious to find fault
with pieces which their author wished to destroy. But it
is not clear that he meant to include in this condemnation
all the articles in this group : especially those on *Johnson*
and *Bacon*, might be supposed excepted, and to come
under the head of those "moral questions" in his treatment of which he did not consider himself to have failed.
They are much more moral studies than literary criticisms.
Now we have had occasion to notice that Macaulay's
insight into character, unless it was exceptionally free from
knots and straight in the grain, was fitful and uncertain.
Neither Johnson nor Bacon were men whom he could
have been expected to see through with a wide and tolerant
eye. With Johnson, Boswell is inseparably associated ;
and Macaulay has spoken of him also with abundant
emphasis. To these three, therefore, our remarks will be
confined.

His paradox about Boswell is well known, and consists
in tracing the excellence of his book to the badness of the
author. Other men, we are told, have attained to literary
eminence in spite of their weaknesses. Boswell attained it
by reason of his weaknesses. " If he had not been a great
fool, he would not have been a great writer." " He had
quick observation and a retentive memory. These qualities,

if he had been a man of sense and virtue would scarcely
have sufficed to make him conspicuous.   But as he was a
dunce, a parasite, and a coxcomb, they have made him
immortal." Sense and virtue have in that case a great
deal to answer for, in depriving the world of masterly
biographies. How it happened that the best of books was
written by the most arrant of fools, Macaulay neglects to
explain. Blind chance, or a fortuitous concourse of
atoms, have been supposed to offer a sufficient account
of the origin of the world : and apparently something
similar was imagined here. Critical helplessness could
hardly go further. Still, although Macaulay habitually
fails to analyze and exhibit the merits of literary work,
he rarely overlooks them. Boswell, he says, had neither
logic, eloquence, wit, learning, taste, nor so much of
the reasoning faculty as to be capable even of sophistry.
"He is always ranting, or twaddling." What then, is
there to praise in his book ? The reports of Johnson's
conversations, and those of the Club, might be the supposed answer. But did Macaulay, so able an artist himself,
think nothing of the great and rare art of *mise en scène* ?
Did he suppose that a shorthand writer's report of those
famous wit-combats would have done as well, or better ?
The fact is, that no dramatist or novelist of the whole century surpassed, or even equalled Boswell, in rounded, clear,
and picturesque presentation—in real dramatic faculty.
Macaulay's attack on his moral character is even more
offensive. He calls him an idolater and a slave ; says he
was like a creeper, which must cling to some stronger
plant ; and that it was only by accident that he did not
fasten himself on Wilkes or Whitfield. Nothing could
be more unjust, more unintelligent. Boswell's attitude to
Johnson, as was so well pointed out by Carlyle, in an

H

article which it is difficult not to regard in some respects
as a covert answer to this of Macaulay's, was one of boundless reverence and love to a superior in intellect and moral
worth. His feeling towards Paoli was of a similar kind.
This fervent hero-worship Macaulay cannot in the least
understand. In his view, it was mere base sycophancy and
toad-eating. Boswell, he says, " was always laying himself
at the feet of some eminent man, and begging to be spit
upon and trampled on." Well might Carlyle say that the
last thing that Boswell would have done, if he had been a
mere flunkey, would have been to act as he did. Johnson
was never of much importance in the great world of fashion,
into which he penetrated very nearly as little at the end as
at the beginning of his career. Boswell could, as a Scotch
Tory of good birth, and an eldest son, easily have found
much more serviceable patrons to whom to pay his court
than the ragged, ill-tempered old scholar, who gave him
many more kicks than halfpence. Macaulay might have
recollected that he himself once paid his court to an insolent
aristocrat, Lady Holland, who ordered her guests about as
if they were footmen ; that though he certainly did not
waste his time in running after obscure sages, he knew
quite well how, by a judicious mixture of independence
and usefulness, to attract the notice of a powerful Minister.
Boswell's faults and vices are obvious enough : but if he
was the insufferable bore and noodle that Macaulay describes, how came Johnson—a man of masculine sense—
to make him his intimate, to spend months with him in
the daily contact of a long journey, and then pronounce
him " the best travelling-companion in the world " ?

We now come to *Johnson*. Besides the article in the
Edinburgh Review, we have the biography published in the
Encyclopedia Britannica, written twenty-five years after-

wards. The latter, as belonging to his last and best manner, is more chaste in language, and more kindly and tolerant in tone than the Essay; still it is essentially on the same lines of thought and sentiment. We have the same clear perception of the external husk of Johnson; but there is as little penetration into his deeper character in the one case as in the other. There is nothing unfair or ungenerous; especially in the biography there seems a fixed resolve to be as generous as possible; but the appreciation is inadequate, and chiefly confined to the surface. The following is nearly Macaulay's masterpiece in superficial portraiture, as showing his tendency to dwell on the outside appearance of character and little besides :—

Johnson grown old—Johnson in the fulness of his fame, and in the enjoyment of a competent fortune, is better known to us than any other man in history. Everything about him—his coat, his wig, his figure, his face, his scrofula, his St. Vitus's dance, his rolling walk, his blinking eye, the outward signs which too clearly marked his approbation of his dinner, his insatiable appetite for fish-sauce and veal pie with plums, his inextinguishable thirst for tea, his trick of touching the posts as he walked, his mysterious practice of treasuring up scraps of orange peel, his morning slumbers, his midnight disputations, his contortions, his mutterings, his gruntings, his puffings, his vigorous, acute, and ready eloquence, his sarcastic wit, his vehement insolence, his fits of tempestuous rage, his queer inmates—old Mr. Levett and blind Mrs. Williams, the cat, Hodge, and negro Frank—all are as familiar to us as objects by which we have been surrounded from our childhood.

There is all through both pieces too much dwelling on Johnson's coarse manners, fits of ill-temper, and tendency to over-eat himself. These details are welcome in a biography, but out of place in a critical estimate. The only point of view from which Johnson can be properly judged is that which Macaulay never took up—the religious point of view. Johnson was an ardent believer, ever fighting with doubt. His heart was full of faith, while his intellect was inclined to scepticism. A great deal of his impatience and irritability arose from this dual condition of his mind and sentiments. He felt that if he listened to unbelief he would be lost. He was always wanting more evidence than he could get for supernatural things. That was why he hunted after the Cock Lane Ghost, and was always fond of stories that seemed to confirm the belief in a life beyond the grave. He disbelieved the earthquake of Lisbon, because it seemed to reflect on the benevolence of God. It is this insecure but ardent piety which gives him an interest and a pathos from which the common run of contented believers are generally free. Next to his piety, the profound tenderness of Johnson's nature is his most marked trait. When they are fused together, as they sometimes were, the result is inexpressibly touching, as in that notice in his diary of the death of his " dear old friend," Catherine Chambers. When we read of his incessant benevolence, we can understand the love he inspired in all who really knew him, which made Goldsmith say, " He has nothing of the bear but the skin ;" and Burke say, when he was out-talked by Johnson to some one's regret, " It is enough for me to have rung the bell for him." These things are not exactly overlooked by Macaulay, but they are not brought out; whereas Johnson's puffings, and gruntings, and perspiration when at his dinner, are made very prominent.

We now come, not without reluctance, to look at the deplorable article on *Bacon*.

The historical portion has only just lately received such

an exposure at the hands of the late Mr. Spedding, that to dwell upon it here is as unnecessary as it would be impertinent.　Two octavo volumes were not found more than sufficient to set forth the full proofs of Macaulay's quite astounding inaccuracies, misrepresentations, and even falsifications of truth.　The only question that we can discuss even for a moment in this place, is what could have been Macaulay's motive for writing with such passion and want of good faith against a man whom in the same breath he extolled even to excess.　We cannot suspect him—"a lump of good nature"—of malignity. The probability is that his usual incapacity to see through an intricate character led him into airing one of those moral paradoxes of which he was fond.　A jarring contrast of incompatible qualities, so far from repelling, very much attracted him in a character.　He seems to have thought it good fun to expand Pope's line into an article of a hundred pages.　One can imagine him thinking as he wrote, "What will they say to this?" for the rest, meaning no particular harm either to Bacon or any one. The piece has no moral earnestness about it, and is flippant in thought even when decorous in language.

The object is a deliberate attack and invective against all higher speculation, which is branded as mere cant and hypocrisy.　The philosophy of both Zeno and Epicurus we are told was a "garrulous, declaiming, canting, wrangling philosophy."　The philosophy of the ancients is pronounced "barren."　The ancient philosophers, in those very matters "for the sake of which they neglected all the vulgar interests of mankind, did nothing, and worse than nothing."　"We know that the philosophers were no better than other men.　From the testimony of friends as well as foes, ... it is plain that these teachers of

virtue had all the vices of their neighbours with the
additional vice of hypocrisy." Religion itself when allied
with philosophy became equally pernicious. The great
merit of Bacon, was that he cleared his mind of all this
rubbish. " He had no anointing for broken bones, no
fine theories *de finibus*, no arguments to persuade men out
of their senses. He knew that men and philosophers, as
well as other men, do actually love life, health, comfort,
honour, security, the society of friends ; and do actually
dislike death, sickness, pain, poverty, disgrace, danger,
separation from those to whom they are attached. He
knew that religion, though it often regulates and modifies
these feelings, seldom eradicates them ; nor did he think
it desirable for mankind that they should be eradicated."
Much more is said against the ancient philosophers, and
in favour of Bacon, who appears moreover to have had
two peculiar merits ; first, that he never meddled with
those enigmas " which have puzzled hundreds of generations, and will puzzle hundreds more "—the grounds of
moral obligation and the freedom of the human will ;
secondly, that he despised speculative theology as much
as he despised speculative philosophy. In short, his
peculiar and extraordinary quality was that he was an
ἰδιώτης, a mere common man, and that is precisely why
he was so great a philosopher. "'It was because he dug
deep that he was able to pile high," deep digging being
apparently the characteristic of the common man.

The point especially deserving of notice in this extraordinary diatribe is, that all spiritual religion is as much
aimed at as philosophy, though the attack is veiled with
great prudence and skill. But every word said against
philosophy would apply equally against religion. Every
sneer and gibe flung at Plato, Zeno, and Epictetus, would

equally serve against Thomas à Kempis, St. Francis of Sales, or Jeremy Taylor. It is not at all easy to determine what could have induced Macaulay to commit this outrage. He is generally excessively observant of the *bienséances*. Was he avenging some old private grudge against a Puritanical education? Had he become convinced that spiritual aspirations were moonshine? There is certainly a vehemence in his onslaught which almost points to a personal injury, as Porson said of Gibbon's attack on Christianity. In any case we must admit that on no other occasion did Macaulay descend so low as on this. Nowhere else has he given us such an insight into the limitations of his heart and understanding, and of his strangely imperfect knowledge, with all his reading. It would require pages, where we have not room for sentences, to expound the matter fully. Take one or two instances, merely because they are short. He reproaches the ancient philosophy with having made no progress in eight hundred years: "Look at the schools of this wisdom four centuries before the Christian era and four centuries after that era. Compare the men whom those schools formed at those two periods. Compare Plato and Libanius; Pericles and Julian. This philosophy confessed, nay boasted, that for every end but one it was useless. Had it attained that one end?" It is difficult to handle the sciolism implied in such remarks and such a question. What had occurred between the dates specified—those of Pericles and Julian? Only the conquest of the world by the Romans, the rise and fall of the Roman Republic and Empire, the invasion of the barbarians, and the proximate dissolution of society. This is to count for nothing. The greatest revolution in human annals—the death throes, in short, of the old world—could not be

expected to influence the course and value of speculation !
The thing to notice was that Libanius was inferior to
Plato, and Julian to Pericles, and that settled the point
that the ancient philosophy was nothing but cant and
hypocrisy.   Again, we are asked to believe that it was
through the perversity of a few great minds that the
blessings of the experimental philosophy were so long
withheld from the world.   The human mind had been
"misdirected ;" "trifles occupied the sharp and vigorous
intellects" of the Greeks and of the schoolmen.   Socrates
and Plato were the chief authors of this evil, which
tainted the whole body of ancient philosophy "from
the time of Plato downwards."   Plato has to bear the
enormous guilt of having "done more than any other
person towards giving the minds of speculative men that
bent which they retained till they received from Bacon a
new impulse in a diametrically opposite direction."   Had
it not been for these lamentable aberrations with which
Macaulay says he has no patience, we should have had,
no doubt, diving-bells, steam-engines, and vaccination in
the time of the Peloponnesian war ; or why not say in
the time of the Trojan war, or even of Noah's ark.   That
society and the human intellect have laws of organic
growth, the stages of which cannot be transposed, any
more than the periods of youth and old age can be
transposed in the life of an individual, was a conception
which never dawned even faintly on Macaulay's mind.
He was as little competent to speak of experimental
science, which he belauded, as of philosophy, which he
vilified.   He says several times in various forms that
science should only be cultivated for its immediate practical
and beneficial results.   He applauds Bacon because "he
valued geometry chiefly if not solely on account of those

uses which to Plato appeared so base," for his love of " those pursuits which *directly* tend to improve the condition of mankind," for the importance ascribed "to those arts which increase the outward comforts of our species ; " and he excuses any over-strength of statement in this matter, by saying that it was an error in the right direction, and that he vastly prefers it to the opposite error of Plato. Now this shows that he failed to grasp the method of science as much as the method and import of philosophy. Science has never prospered until it has freed itself from bondage to the immediate wants of life—till it has pursued its investigations with perfect indifference as to the results and uses to which they may be applied.   But it is needless to pursue the subject.   The effect of the whole article is the same as that produced by a man of rude manners making his way into a refined and well-bred company ; with an unbecoming carriage and a loud voice he goes up to the dignified dames—the ancient Philosophies one after another—and asks them what they do there ; mocks at their fine ways ; and finishes by telling them roundly that in his opinion they are all no better than they should be.   Nothing that Macaulay has written has been more injurious to his fame as a serious thinker.

Nevertheless, say what we will, Macaulay's essays remain a brilliant and fascinating page in English literature. The world is never persistently mistaken in such cases. Time enough has elapsed, since their publication, to submerge them in oblivion had they not contained a vital spark of genius which criticism is powerless to extinguish. If not wells of original knowledge, they have acted like irrigating rills which convey and distribute the fertilizing waters from the fountain-head.   The best would adorn any literature, and even the less successful have a pic-

turesque animation, and convey an impression of power
that will not easily be matched.   And again we need
to bear in mind that they were the productions of a
writer immersed in business, written in his scanty moments
of leisure when most men would have rested or sought
recreation.   Macaulay himself was most modest in his
estimate of their value, and resisted their republication as
long as he could.   It was the public that insisted on
their reissue, and few would be bold enough to deny that
the public was right.

CHAPTER IV.

NARRATIVE OF MACAULAY'S LIFE RESUMED UP TO THE
APPEARANCE OF THE HISTORY.

(A.D. 1841—1848.)

"Sir,' said Dr. Johnson, "it is wonderful how little
Garrick assumes. No, sir, Garrick *fortunam reverenter
habuit.* Then, sir, Garrick did not find, but made his
way to the tables, the levees, and almost the bed-chambers of the great. If all this had happened to me, I
should have had a couple of fellows with long poles walking before me to knock down everybody that stood in the
way." One is reminded of these wise and kindly words
from the rough but tender-hearted old moralist when
reflecting on the uniform success and prosperity which
attended Macaulay in everything he undertook. With
the single exception of his failing to secure a place in the
Tripos at Cambridge, which, after all, had no evil effects,
as he obtained a fellowship notwithstanding, he did not put
his hand to a thing without winning loud applause. In
his story there are no failures to record. The trials and
straitened means of his early years arose from no fault of
his. As soon as he began to rebuild the shattered fortunes
of his family, the work went on without break or interruption, and was triumphantly accomplished before he
had reached his fortieth year. But he had done much

more than restore his material circumstances ; in the meanwhile he had acquired a wide and brilliant fame.   He had
made his way to the tables, the levees, and bed-chambers
of the great.   A *novus homo*, he was treated with the distinction which in our aristocratic society was at that time
nearly always reserved for the so called " well-born."   And
yet he, like Garrick, bore his honours, if not meekly, yet
without a particle of insolence or assumption, or the least
symptom that his head had been turned.   And this was
the result not of religious or philosophic discipline, of a
conscious moral cultivation of humility, and a sober spirit,
but of mere sweetness of nature and constitutional
amiability.

   After his fall, or, perhaps we should say, his rise from
office, he almost immediately proceeded to tempt fortune
in a very perilous way.   He put forth a volume of poems
—the *Lays of Ancient Rome*.   His eyes were quite open
to the risk.   To Napier, who had expressed doubts about
the venture, he wrote :—

   I do not wonder at your misgivings.   I should have felt
similar misgivings if I had learned that any person, however
distinguished by talents and knowledge, whom I knew as a
writer only by prose works, was about to publish a volume of
poetry—had I seen advertised a poem by Mackintosh, by
Dugald Stewart, or even by Burke, I should have augured
nothing but failure ; and I am far from putting myself on a
level with the least of the three.

Few writers have surpassed Macaulay in that most useful
of all gifts, a clear and exact knowledge of the reach and
nature of his talents.   It never stood him in better stead
than on the present occasion.

   It will be remembered that he was engaged on the lay

of *Horatius* when he was in Italy.   But he had written
two lays while in India, and submitted them to Dr. Arnold
of Rugby, who had spoken of them with high praise.
The subject had thus been a long time in his mind, and
the composition, though no doubt often interrupted, had
been most careful and deliberate.   Macaulay had the faculty
of rhyme in no common degree, and he was also a scientific prosodian.   He consulted his friends about his verses,
and, what was less common, he took their advice when
they pointed out defects.   Several years off and on, thus
employed on four poems, which together do not amount
to two-thirds of *Marmion*, were a guarantee against hasty
work ; and the result corresponds.   The versification of
the Lays is technically without blemish, and this correctness has been purchased by no sacrifice of vigour.   On the
contrary, Macaulay's prose at its best is not so terse as his
verse.   He had naturally a tendency to declamation.   In
the Lays this tendency is almost entirely suppressed, as if
the greater intensity of thought needed for metrical composition had consumed the wordy undergrowth of rhetoric,
and lifted him into a clearer region where he saw the facts
with unimpeded vision.   On the other hand, it must be
admitted that the rhythm is somewhat monotonous and
mechanical.   The melody never wanders spontaneously
into new and unexpected modulation, and seems rather
the result of care and labour than a natural gift of music.
Some lines are strangely harsh, as —

So spun she, and so sang she,

a concourse of sibilants which can hardly be spoken, and
would have shocked a musical ear.

But the Lays have, nevertheless, very considerable poetical merit, on which it is the more necessary to dwell, as there

appears to be disposition in some quarters to only grudgingly allow it, or even to deny it. The marked taste of intelligent children for Macaulay's poems is not to be undervalued. It shows, as Mr. Maurice said, that there was something fresh, young, and unsophisticated in the mind of the writer. But Macaulay has no reason to fear a more critical tribunal. There is a directness of presentation in his best passages, the poetical result is so independent of any artifice of language, or laboured pomp of diction, but, on the contrary, arises so naturally from mere accuracy of drawing and clear vision of the fact, that the question is not whether his work is good, but whether in its kind it has often been surpassed. Mr. Ruskin insists strongly on "the peculiar dignity possessed by all passages which limit their expression to the pure fact, and leave the hearer to gather what he can from it." [1] This acknowledged sign of strength is very frequent in Macaulay's Lays. Few writers indulge less in the Pathetic Fallacy than he. Line after line contains nothing but the most simple statement of fact in quite unadorned language. For instance :—

> But with a crash like thunder
> Fell every loosened beam,
> And, like a dam, the mighty wreck
> Lay right athwart the stream;
> And a long shout of triumph
> Rose from the walls of Rome,
> As to the highest turret-tops
> Was splashed the yellow foam.

Every statement here might be made with propriety by a simple man, as, e.g. a carpenter who had witnessed the event—the noise of the falling fabric, its position in the river, the exulting shout which naturally followed, the

[1] *Modern Painters,* vol. iii. c. 12.

splash of *yellow* foam—no otiose epithet, as the Tiber was the stream.   Each line might form part of a bald report, and yet the whole is graphic simply because it is literally true.   The art, like all art, of course consists in seeing and seizing the right facts and giving them prominence. Macaulay's power of drawing, at once accurate and characteristic, gives to his descriptions at times a sharpness of outline which seems borrowed from sculpture :—

> Round turned he, as not deigning
>   Those craven ranks to see ;
> Nought spake he to Lars Porsena ;
>   To Sextus nought spake he.
> But he saw on Palatinus
>   The white porch of his home,
> And he spake to the noble river
>   That rolls by the towers of Rome.
>
> " Oh Tiber ! father Tiber !
>   To whom the Romans pray,
> A Roman's life, a Roman's arms,
>   Take thou in charge this day ! "
> *So he spake, and speaking sheathed*
>   *The good sword by his side,*
> *And with his harness on his back*
>   *Plunged headlong in the tide.*

Is there not a definite objectiveness of presentation here almost statuesque ?

Macaulay's calmness and self-restraint in verse are very marked as compared with the opposite qualities which he sometimes displays in prose.   Occasionally he reaches a note of tragic solemnity without effort, and by the simplest means, as in the visions which haunted Sextus :—

> Lavinium and Laurentum
>   Had on the left their post,
> With all the banners of the marsh,
>   And banners of the coast.

Their leader was false Sextus
　　That wrought the deed of shame;
With restless pace and haggard face
　　To his last field he came.
Men said he saw strange visions
　　Which none beside might see,
And that strange sounds were in his ears
　　Which none might hear but he.
A woman fair and stately,
　　But pale as are the dead,
Oft through the watches of the night
　　Sat spinning by his bed.
And as she plied the distaff,
　　In a sweet voice and low
She sang of great old houses,
　　And fights fought long ago.
So spun she, and so sang she,
　　Until the East was grey,
Then pointed to her bleeding breast,
　　And shrieked, and fled away.

But his poetical merit, considerable as it was, is not the
most important and interesting feature in the *Lays of
Ancient Rome*. In literary classification Macaulay of
course belongs to what is called the romantic school; he
could not do otherwise, living when he did. He was five
years old when the *Lay of the Last Minstrel* was published,
and he received in the impressionable period of youth the
full impact of the Waverley novels. We have already seen
how much they contributed to form his notions of history.
It was not likely when he took to writing ballads that the
influence of Scott would be less than when he wrote prose.
Accordingly we meet with a reminiscence and echo of
Scott all through the lays. This was unavoidable, and
Macaulay seeks in no wise to disguise the fact. On the
other hand, no one could resemble Scott less in his deeper
sympathies and cast of mind than Macaulay. Scott had

the instinct of a wild animal for the open air, the forest,
the hill-side. He—

> Loved nature like a horned cow,
> Deer or bird or carribou;

and thought that if he did not see the heatner once a year
he should die. Macaulay was a born *citadin*, and cared for
nature hardly at all. His sister doubted whether any scenery
ever pleased him so much as his own Holly Lodge, or Mr.
Thornton's garden at Battersea Rise. Scott, again, was
full of the romantic spirit. His mind dwelt by preference
on the past, which was lovely to him. Macaulay had an
American belief and delight in modern material progress,
and was satisfied that no age in the past was ever as good
as the present. Scott's notions of politics were formed
on the feudal pattern. He could understand and admire
fealty, the devotion of vassal to lord, the personal attach-
ment of clansman to his chief, but of the reasoned obedience
and loyalty of the citizen to the state, to the polity of
which he forms a part, Scott seems as good as unconscious.
It would not be easy to quote, from his poems at least, a
passage which implied any sympathy with civil duty and
sacrifice to the *res publica*, to the common weal. As Mr.
Ruskin says, his sympathies are rather with outlaws and
rebels, especially under the "greenwood tree," and he has
but little objection to rebellion even to a king, provided
it be on private and personal grounds, and not systematic
or directed to great public aims. This was the genuine
feudal spirit which ignored the state and the correlated
notion of citizenship, and trusted for social cohesion to
the fragile tie of the liegeman's sworn fidelity to his suze-
rain. Nothing stirred Scott's blood more than military
prowess, the conflict of armed men, but he remains con-

I

tented with the conflict ; he cares little in what cause men
fight, so long as they do fight and accomplish "deeds of
arms." It may be for love, or the point of honour, or
because the chief commands it, or merely for the luxury
of exchanging blows ; but for the patriotic valour which
fights for hearth and home, and native city, he has hardly
a word to say.

On opening Macaulay's Lays we find ourselves in a world
which is the exact opposite of this ;—civic patriotism, zeal
for the public weal whether against foreign foe or domestic
tyrant—these are his sources of inspiration. And there
is thus a curious contrast, almost contradiction, between
the outward form of the poems and their contents. The
real romantic ballad and its modern imitations, properly
refer to times in which the notion of a State, composed of
citizens who support it on reasoned grounds, has not emerged.
The *polis* is not to be found in Homer, or in *Chevy Chase*, or
in Scott. In Macaulay's ballads the State is everything.
His love for ordered civil life, his zeal for the abstract
idea of government instituted for the well-being of all who
live under it, are as intense in him as they were in the
breast of Pericles. Thus the key-note of the ballads is as
remote as possible from that of Scott, and indeed of all
mediævalists, and not only remote, but very much nobler.
The fighting in the lays does not arise from mere reckless
light-hearted ferocity--

> That marked the foeman's feudal hate,

but from lofty social union which leads the brave to self-
sacrifice for the common good.

> For Romans in Rome's quarrel
> Spared neither land nor gold,
> Nor son nor wife, nor limb nor life
> In the brave days of old.

And this higher moral strain has its poetic reward. Macaulay attains a heroism of sentiment, which Scott never reaches. Compare the almost effeminate sob over James killed at Flodden :—

> He saw the wreck his rashness wrought,
> Reckless of life he desperate fought,
>   And fell on Flodden plain.
> And well in death his trusty brand
> Firm clenched within his manly hand
>   Beseemed the monarch slain ;
> But O! how changed since yon blithe night,
> Gladly I turn me from the sight
>   Unto my tale again.

Compare this with the exultant and fiery joy over the death of Valerius.

XVIII.

> But fiercer grew the fighting
>   Around Valerius dead ;
> For Titus dragged him by the foot
>   And Aulus by the head.
> "On, Latines, on!" quoth Titus,
>   "See how the rebels fly !"
> "Romans, stand firm," quoth Aulus,
>   "And win this fight or die.
> They must not give Valerius
>   To raven and to kite ;
> For aye Valerius loathed the wrong,
>   And aye upheld the right ;
> And for your wives and babies
>   In the front rank he fell.
> Now play the men for the good house
>   That loves the people well."

XIX.

> Then tenfold round the body
>   The roar of battle rose,
> Like the roar of a burning forest
>   When a strong north wind blows.

Now backward, and now forward,
    Rocked furiously the fray,
Till none could see Valerius,
    And none wist where he lay.
For shivered arms and ensigns
    Were heaped there in a mound,
And corpses stiff, and dying men
    That writhed and gnawed the ground ;
And wounded horses kicking,
    And snorting purple foam :
*Right well did such a couch befit
    A consular of Rome.*

Macaulay had thoroughly assimilated the lofty civic
spirit of the ancients—a spirit which was seriously injured
when not wholly destroyed in the Middle Ages by Feudalism and Catholicism together.

The lay of *Virginia* is of less even and sustained excellence than the two lays which precede it. The speech of
Icilius and the description of the tumult which followed
are admirable for spirit and vigour. It may be noticed
generally that Macaulay is always very successful in his
descriptions of excited crowds—he does it *con amore*—he
had none of the disdain for the multitude which Carlyle
manifests in and out of season. On this occasion the
liberal politician combined with the artist to produce a
powerful effect. He had a noble hatred of tyranny, and
his sympathies were wholly with the many as against the
few. There was a righteous fierceness in him at the sight
of wrong, which is the stuff of which true patriots in
troubled times are made.

And thrice the tossing Forum set up a frightful yell ;
" See, see, thou dog ! what thou hast done, and hide thy shame
    in hell,
Thou that wouldst make our maidens slaves must first make
    slaves of men.
Tribunes ! hurrah for Tribunes ! Down with the wicked ten !"

This speech of Icilius is no closet rhetoric composed by a man who had never addressed a mob; it is the speech of a practised orator who knows how to rouse passion and set men's hearts on fire. It is also a thoroughly dramatic speech; good in itself, but made much better by the situation of the supposed speaker. From a modern point of view it is better than the speech which Livy makes Icilius deliver, with its references to Roman law. On the other hand, the speech of Virginius to his daughter, just before he stabs her, is quite as bad as that of Icilius is good. It is a singular thing that Macaulay, whose sensibility and genuine tenderness of nature are quite beyond doubt, had almost no command of the pathetic. The explanation seems to be that he really was too sensitive. He says in his diary : " I generally avoid novels which are said to have much pathos. The suffering which they produce is to me a very real suffering, and of that I have quite enough without them." The fact, though highly creditable to his heart, shows a marked limitation of range, and excludes him from the class of artists by nature, who are at once susceptible and masters of emotion. Feeling must have subsided into serene calm before it can be successfully embodied in art. In any case Macaulay seems to have been unusually incapable of, or averse to, the expression of tender and pathetic sentiment. He has in his correspondence and diaries more than once occasion to refer to the deaths of friends whom we know he loved, and he always does so in a curiously awkward manner, as if he were ashamed of his feelings, and wished to hide them even from himself. "Jeffrey is gone, dear fellow ; I loved him as much as it is easy to love a man who belongs to an older generation. . . . . After all dear Jeffrey's death is hardly a matter for mourning." He had been on

terms of affectionate intimacy with Jeffrey for more than
twenty-five years. On hearing that Harry Hallam was
dying at Sienna, he says, "What a trial for my dear old
friend " (the historian) ; "I feel for the lad himself, too.
Much distressed, I dined however. We dine unless the
blow comes very very near the heart indeed." There is
evidently a deliberate avoidance of giving way to the
expression of grief. And yet when he comes across some
of his sister Margaret's letters twenty-two years after her
death, he is overcome, and bursts into tears. Macaulay
could not hold the more passionate emotions sufficiently at
arm's length to describe them properly when he felt them.
And when they were passed, his imagination did not
reproduce them with a clearness available for art. A man
on the point of stabbing his daughter to save her from
dishonour would certainly not think of making the stagey
declamation which Macaulay has put into the mouth of
Virginius. The frigid conceits about "Capua's marble
halls," and the kite gloating upon his prey, are the last
things that would occur to a mind filled with such awful
passions. Macaulay would have done better on this occasion to copy the impressive brevity of Livy, "Hoc te uno,
quo possum modo, filia in libertatem vindico." If it be
said that the object was not historical or even poetical
verisimilitude, but to write an exciting ballad such as
might be supposed to stir the contemporaries of Licinius
and Sextius, the answer will be given presently in reference
to a parallel but much simpler case.

  The Prophecy of Capys is distinctly languid as a whole,
though it has some fine stanzas, and contains one of the
most delicate touches of colour that Macaulay ever laid on:—

> And Venus loves the whispers
>   Of plighted youth and maid,

> In April's ivory moonlight
> Beneath the chestnut's shade.

The unclouded moon of Italy lighting up the limestone rocks produces just the nuance of green ivory. Generally his sense of colour is weak compared with Scott, whose eye for colour is such that while reading him we seem to be gazing on the purple glory of the hills when the heather is in bloom : Macaulay is grey and dun. It is curious to compare how Macaulay and Scott deal with the same situation, that of a person anxiously watching for the appearance of another. Scott does it by putting the sense of sight on the alert :—

> The noble dame on turret high,
> Who waits her gallant knight,
> Looks to the western beam to spy
> *The flash of armour bright;*
> The village maid with hand on brow
> The level ray to shade,
> Upon the footpath watches now
> *For Colin's darkening plaid.*

Macaulay puts the sense of hearing on guard.

> Since the first gleam of daylight,
> Sempronius had not ceased
> *To listen for the rushing*
> Of horse-hoofs from the east.

A keen sense of colour is the peculiar note, one might say the badge of the romantic school, and this is true even of musicians (compare Handel, Bach, Haydn, with Beethoven, Schumann, and Wagner). It is not without interest that we find Macaulay a sort of forced disciple of the romantic school, differing from it in this as well as in the other peculiarities above mentioned.

The Prophecy of Capys suggests a sense of fatigue and

flagging inspiration in the writer which are not without a
certain significance, and may help to throw light on a
question which has a certain interest for some persons.
The question is whether Macaulay should be considered a
poet or not. " Some fastidious critics," says Mr. Trevelyan, " think it proper to deny him that title." Now,
if by this is meant that he not only was no poet but wrote
no poetry, the statement is obviously excessive and unfair.
To have written poetry does not necessarily constitute
a man a poet. We need to know before according that
title to a man, what relative proportion the poetic vein
bore to the rest of his nature ; how far poetry was his
natural and spontaneous mode of utterance. It is evident
that quantity as well as quality has to be considered.
Should we consider the writer of the best sonnet that ever
was written a poet, if he never had written anything else ?
Was Single-speech Hamilton an orator ? When Johnson
called Gray a " barren rascal," he implied in coarse language
a truth of some importance, and passed a just criticism on
Gray. Facile abundance is not necessarily a merit in itself,
but it at least points to natural fertility of the soil, and its
adaptation to the crop produced. On the other hand, rare
exotics painfully reared by artificial means, have not often
more than a fancy value. Shelley writing the twelve books
of the *Revolt of Islam* in a few months, Byron writing the
first canto of *Don Juan* in a few weeks, showed by so
doing that poetry was the spontaneous product of their
minds, that the labour was small compared with the greatness of the result, and that in short the natural richness of
the soil was the cause of their fertility. From this point
of view it is manifest that Macaulay was no poet, though
certainly he has written poetry. Directed by an immense
knowledge of literature and a cultivated taste,—by watch-

ing for the movements of inspiration, by the careful storage of every raindrop that fell from the clouds of fancy, he collected a small vessel full of clear limpid water, the sparkling brightness of which it is unjust not to acknowledge. But the process was too slow and laborious to justify us in calling him a poet. What a different gale impelled him when he wrote prose : he has only to shake out the sheet, and his sails become concave and turgid with the breeze. That is to say, prose was his vocation, poetry was not. But that is no reason why we should not admire *Horatius* as one of the best ballads in the language. As Lessing wrote dramas by dint of critical acumen, without, according to his own conviction, any natural dramatic talent, so Macaulay wrote two or three graceful poems by the aid of great culture and trained literary taste.

A question was left unanswered on a former page, and reference was made to a parallel case. The question was, whether such a lay as that of *Virginia* was in any degree more likely to represent an original lost lay written at the time of the Licinian Rogations, than one written at the Decemvirate. One of Macaulay's best ballads after the *Lays* may help us to answer the question. *The Battle of Ivry*, though not so careful and finished in language as the *Lays* is equal to any of them in fire. It is full also of what is called local colour and those picturesque touches which delight the admirers of the pseudo-antique. Now it happens that we have a Huguenot lay on this very subject, and it is interesting to compare the genuine article with the modern imitation. The romance and chivalry which Macaulay, following the taste of his time, has infused into his ballad, are entirely wanting in the Huguenot song, which is very little more than a dull

and somewhat fierce hymn with a s trong Old Testament
flavour.   In the modern poem the real local colour, the
real sentiments with which a Huguenot regarded the
defeat of the League are omitted, and replaced by picturesque and graceful sentiments, against which the only
thing to be said is that they are entirely wanting in historical fidelity and truth.   Even matters of fact are
incorrectly given.   No one would infer from Macaulay's
ballad that Henry IV.'s army contained the flower of the
French nobility, Catholic as well as Protestant, and as for
the "lances" and "thousand spears in rest" with which
he arms Henry's knights, it was one of the latter's military
innovations to have suppressed and replaced them by sabres
and pistols, far more efficacious weapons at close quarters.
But the romantic, chivalrous, and joyous tone is that which
most contrasts with the gloomy, religious spirit of the
original.   The song is supposed to be made in the name
of Henry of Navarre, who gives all the glory to God.
Two or three stanzas out of twenty will be sufficient to
quote :—

> Je chante ton honneur sous l'effect de mes armes,
> A ta juste grandeur je rapporte le tout,
> Car, du commencement du milieu jusqu'au bout,
> Toy seul m'as guaranty au plus fort des allarmes.
>
> Du plus haut de ton Ciel regardant en la terre,
> Méprisant leur audace et des graves sourcis,
> Desdaignant ces mutins, soudain tu les as mis
> Au plus sanglant malheur que sceut porter la guerre.
>
> Le jour cesse plustost que la chasse ne cesse ;
> Tout ce camp désolé ne se peut asseurer,
> Et à peine la nuict les laisse respirer,
> Car les miens courageux les poursuyvoyent sans cesse.[2]

---

[2] Le Chansonnier Huguenot, du xvie siècle, vol. ii., p. 315.

So we see that the chivalrous humanitarian sentiments
which Macaulay has put in the mouth of his Huguenot
bard are without foundation.

> But out spake gentle Henry, " No Frenchman is my foe ;
> Down, down with every foreigner, but let your brethren go."
> Oh ! was there ever such a knight, in friendship or in war,
> As our sovereign lord, King Henry, the soldier of Navarre ?

" Beaucoup de fantassins français furent néanmoins sabrés
ou arquebusés dans la première fureur de la victoire ! la
déroute fut au moins aussi sanglante que le combat." Now
the question mooted was as to the probability of these
ballads having any historical fidelity or verisimilitude.
With regard to a ballad not three hundred years old, we
find one of them has none. What is the probability of
those which pretend to go back a good deal over two
thousand years being more accurate ?

And this brings us to the consideration of the question
whether we can honestly compliment and congratulate
Macaulay on his *Lays of Ancient Rome.* The preceding
remarks, it is hoped, show no tendency to morose hyper-
criticism. But does it raise one's opinion of Macaulay's
earnest sincerity of mind to find him devoting some considerable time to the production of what he candidly
admitted to be but trifles, though "scholarlike and not in-
elegant trifles." He could very well lay his finger on the
defects of Bulwer's *Last Days of Pompeii :* "It labours," he
says, "under the usual faults of all works in which it is
attempted to give moderns a glimpse of ancient manners.
After all, between us and them, there is a great gulf
which no learning will enable a man to clear." At the
very time he made this entry in his journal he was composing his lay on *Horatius,* a much more difficult task

than Bulwer's, for our knowledge of Roman manners under
the empire may be said to be intimate and exact as
compared with our knowledge of Roman manners in the
semi-mythic period of the early republic.   Was it a worthy
occupation for a serious scholar to spend his time in producing mere fancy pictures which could have no value
beyond a certain prettiness, " in the prolongation from age
to age of romantic historical descriptions instead of sifted
truth ? " [3]   Could we imagine Grote or Mommsen, or
Ranke or Freeman engaged in such a way without a certain
sense of degradation ?   This is not making much of a small
matter ; it is really important, reaching down if you consider it well to the deeper elements of character and
primary motive.   Macaulay's love and pursuit of truth,
which he imagined to be dominant passions with him,
were relatively feeble.   The subject has already been
referred to.   It is strange to see how much he deceived
himself on this point.   In the ambitious and wordy verses
he composed on the evening of his defeat at Edinburgh,
he feigns that all the Fairies passed his cradle by, without
a blessing, except the Fairy Queen of Knowledge ; and
she, the " mightest and the best," pronounced—

Yes ; thou wilt love me with exceeding love.

And the three illustrious predecessors whom in this particular he wishes most to resemble, and who are alone
mentioned are the three oddly chosen names of Bacon,
Hyde, and Milton, in all of whom we may confidently
say that the love of truth was *not* the prominent and
striking feature of their character and genius.   Of Bacon,
Macaulay himself has rather overstated, while he deplored,
the weakness of his love of truth as compared to his love of

[3] *Modern Painters,* vol. iii. c. 6.

place and honours.   What Hyde has to do in such company
more than other statesmen, ancient or modern, it is difficult to see.   And in what way did Milton show a love of
truth more than any other poet ?   Macaulay's notion of the
sentiment he claimed, seems to have been abundantly vague.
Kepler verifying his laws and going over the calculations
one hundred and fifty times, in the meanwhile writing
almanacks to keep him from starving ; Newton working
out his theory of gravitation for years, and modestly putting
it aside because the erroneous data on which he calculated
led to incorrect results, then on corrected data writing the
Principia ; nay, Franklin running an unknown risk of his
life by identifying by means of his kite electricity with
lightning, and countless other loyal servants of science
might have been cited with relevancy as types of lovers
of truth.   It is a misuse of language to confuse a general
love of literature, or a very sensible zeal in getting up the
materials for historical scene-painting, with the stern resolution which lays siege to nature's secrets, and will not desist
till they are surrendered.   But such pains are undertaken
only at the bidding of a passionate desire for an answer
by minds which can perceive the test-problems which
have not yet capitulated, but which must be reduced before
any further advance into the Unknown can be safely made.
It is a peculiarity of Macaulay's mind that he rarely sees
problems, that he is not stopped by difficulties out of
which he anxiously seeks an issue.   We never find him
wondering with suspended judgment in what direction
his course may lie.   On the contrary, he has seldom any
doubt or difficulty about anything, his mind is always
made up, and he has a prompt answer for every question.
We may without scruple say that the course of a genuine
love of truth has never run so smooth.   Here was the

early history of Rome full of difficulties which clamoured
for further research and elucidation. The subject had been
just sufficiently worked to whet the curiosity and interest
of an inquiring mind. There were not many men in Europe
more fitted by classical attainments to take the problems
suggested in hand, and advance them a stage nearer to a
correct solution. Macaulay did not consider the matter
in this light at all. To have written a scholarlike essay on
early Roman history would have been to write for a few
score readers in the English and German universities. The
love of truth which he imagined that he possessed would
have directed him into that course. But if he had taken
it, his biographer would most certainly not have been able
to inform us of anything so imposing as this :—" eighteen
thousand of the *Lays of Ancient Rome* were sold in ten
years, forty thousand in twenty years, and by June, 1875,
upwards of a hundred thousand copies had passed into the
hands of readers."

Macaulay did not after leaving office avail himself of his
leisure to resume his interrupted history with the zeal and
promptitude that might have been expected. Besides
the *Lays*, he allowed other and even less important things
to waste his time. He was by no means so resolute in
resisting the blandishments of society as he should have
been, and as he afterwards became. " I have had so much
time occupied by politics and by the society which at this
season fills London that I have written nothing for some
weeks," he wrote to Macvey Napier. He would have shown
more robustness of character and a more creditable absorp-
tion in his work, if he had courageously renounced for
good and all both society and politics, now that he
was for the first time in his life free to devote all his ener-
gies to a great work. Instead of that he loitered for fully

three years before he threw himself with passionate single-hearted concentration on his history.   This shows that the book after all was not generated in the deeper and more earnest parts of his nature, but came mostly from the fancy and understanding.   Or perhaps we should not be very wrong if we surmise that depth and earnestness were somewhat wanting in him.   He had no latent heat of sustained enthusiasm either scientific, political, or artistic.   By a vigorous spurt he could write a brilliant article, which rarely required more than a few weeks.   His ambition, which, like all his passions, was moderate and amiable, was largely satisfied by the very considerable honours which he acquired by his contributions to the blue and yellow *Review ;* he had none of the fierce and relentless thirst for a great fame which drives some men into wrapt isolation, where they are free to nurse and indulge their moods of creative passion.   Neither was he under the dominion of a great thought which hedges a man with solitude even in a crowd.   On the other hand, it is only just to remember that the pressure put upon him to leave his work was severe.   Both in Parliament and the *Edinburgh Review,* he was able to render services which were not likely to be foregone, by those who needed them, without a hard struggle.   For nearly twenty years the quarterly organ of the Whigs had enjoyed a new lease of popularity and power through his contributions.   In the House of Common the beaten and dejected Whigs were grateful beyond words for the welcome aid of his brilliant and destructive oratory.   Mr. Napier appears to have been inconsiderately importunate for articles, and Macaulay, though protesting that he must really now devote himself to his history, with amiable weakness ends by giving in and writing.   But the sacrifice was really too great, and he ought to have seen that it was. He did at last, and resolutely

putting his foot down, declared that he would write no
more for the *Review* till he had brought out two volumes
of his book. He wrote to Napier :—

I hope that you will make your arrangements for some
three or four numbers without counting on me. I find it
absolutely necessary to concentrate my attention on my historical work. You cannot conceive how difficult I find it to do
two things at a time. Men are differently made. Southey
used to work regularly two hours a day on the *History of
Brazil ;* then an hour for the *Quarterly Review ;* then an hour
on the *Life of Wesley;* then two hours on the *Peninsular
War ;* then an hour on the *Book of the Church.* I cannot do
so. I get into the stream of my narrative, and am going along
as smoothly and quickly as posssible. Then comes the necessity
of writing for the *Review.* I lay my *History* aside ; and, when
after some weeks I resume it, I have the greatest difficulty in
recovering the interrupted train of thought. *But for the
Review, I should already have brought out two volumes at
least.* I must really make a resolute effort, or my plan will
end as our poor friend Mackintosh's ended.

This self-reproach and this comparison with Mackintosh
are constantly flowing from his pen.

Another paper from me is at present out of the question.
One in half a year is the utmost of which I can hold out any
hopes. I ought to give my whole leisure to my *History ;* and
fear that if I suffer myself to be diverted from that design, as I
have done, I shall be like poor Mackintosh, leave behind me the
character of a man who would have done something, if he had
concentrated his powers instead of frittering them away. . . .
I must not go on dawdling and reproaching myself all my
life.

This sacrifice to editorial importunity was the more
regrettable as articles, written under this pressure, with

one exception, have added little to Macaulay's fame. The fact is in nowise surprising. Task-work of this kind, even though undertaken at the bidding of friendship, is apt to betray a want both of maturity and spontaneous inspiration. Saving the article on Chatham, a subject which lay in the course of his studies, and with which he took great pains, writing it over three times, Macaulay's contributions to the *Edinburgh* at this period have largely the characteristics of what are vulgarly called " pot-boilers," though in his case they were written to keep, not his own but another man's pot boiling. The articles on Madame D'Arblay's *Memoirs* and on Frederick the Great are thin, crude, perfunctory, and valueless, except as first-rate padding for a periodical review. In the latter he cannot even spell the name of the Principality of Frederick's favourite sister Wilhelmina correctly ; always writing Bareuth instead of Baireuth ; it is but a small error, but it indicates haste, as he was usually careful in the orthography of proper names. But there are worse faults than this. When off his guard, especially when contemptuous or angry, Macaulay easily lapsed into an uncurbed vehemence of language which bordered on vulgarity.

Frederick by no means relinquished his hereditary privilege of kicking and cudgelling. His practice, however, as to that matter, differed in some important respects from his father's. To Frederick William, the mere circumstance that any person whatever, men, women or children, Prussians or foreigners, were within reach of his toes or his cane, appeared to be a sufficient reason for proceeding to belabour them. Frederick required provocation, as well as vicinity.

Again, "The resistance opposed to him by the tribunals inflamed him to fury. He reviled the Chancellor ; he

kicked the shins of his judges." Of Voltaire's skill in
flattery, he remarks :—"And it was only from his hand
that so much sugar could be swallowed without making the
swallower sick." In the article on Madame D'Arblay,
her German colleague, Madame Schwellenberg, is described with a coarseness of tone worthy of the original :
" a hateful old toad-eater, as illiterate as a chamber-maid,
and proud as a whole German chapter." Madame
Schwellenberg "raved like a maniac in the incurable
ward of Bedlam." Madame Schwellenberg "raged like a
wild cat."

Macaulay never fully appreciated the force of modera-
tion, the impressiveness of calm understatement, the
penetrating power of irony. His nature was essentially
simple and not complex ; when a strong feeling arose in
his mind, it came forth at once naked and unashamed ;
it met with no opposition from other feelings capable of
modifying or restraining it. A great deal of his clearness
springs from this single, uninvolved character of his
emotions, which never blend in rich, polyphonic chords,
filling the ear of the mind. Somewhat of this simplicity
appears to have been reflected in his countenance.
Carlyle, who was practically acquainted with a very
different internal economy, once observed Macaulay's face
in repose, as he was turning over the pages of a book.
" I noticed," he said, "the homely Norse features that
you find everywhere in the Western Isles, and I thought
to myself, ' Well, any one can see that you are an honest,
good sort of fellow, made out of oatmeal !'" He resembled
the straight-splitting pine, rather than the gnarled oak. To
liken a woman on account of her ill-temper to a raving
maniac and a wild cat excited in him no qualms; the epithets
expressed his feelings, but no counter wave of fastidious

taste surged up compelling a recast of the whole expression.

It is some confirmation of a view already advanced in these pages that Macaulay's natural aptitude was rather oratorical than literary, that at this very time he was making some of his best speeches in Parliament. The fine literary sense of nuance, the scrupulous choice of epithet, the delicacy which it alarmed by loud tones and colours, in short, the qualities most rare and precious in a writer, are out of place in oratory, which is never more effective than when inspired by manly and massive emotion, enforcing broad and simple conclusions. It is impossible to read Macaulay's speeches without feeling that in delivering them he was wielding an instrument of which he was absolutely the master. The luminous order and logical sequence of the parts are only surpassed by the lofty unity and coherence of the whole. High statesmanlike views are unfolded in language that is at once terse, chaste, and familiar, never fine-drawn or over-subtle, but plain, direct, and forcible, exactly suited to an audience of practical men. Above all, the noble and generous sentiment, which burns and glows through every sentence, melts the whole mass of argument, illustration, and invective into a torrent of majestic oratory, which is as far above the eloquence of rhetoric as high poetry is above the mere rhetoric of verse. It is the more necessary to dwell on this point with some emphasis, as an unjust and wholly unfounded impression seems to be gaining ground that Macaulay was a mere closet orator, who delivered carefully prepared essays in the House of Commons, brilliant perhaps, but unpractical rhetorical exercises that smelt strongly of the lamp. The truth is that Macaulay is never less rhetorical, in the bad sense of the word, than in his speeches. He put on no gloves, he took in hand no buttoned foil, when on well-chosen occasions he came down to the House to make a speech. Blows straight from the shoulder; a short and sharp Roman sword wielded with equal skill and vigour are rather the images suggested by his performance in these conflicts. Yet a hundred persons know his essays for one who is acquainted with his speeches. During the period comprised in this chapter—from 1841 to 1848—he made twelve speeches, and if the world's judgments were dictated by reason and insight instead of fashion and hearsay, no equal portion of Macaulay's works would be deemed so valuable. It is no exaggeration to say that as an orator he moves in a higher intellectual plane than he does as a writer. As a writer he rather avoids the discussion of principles, and is not always happy when he does engage in it. In his speeches we find him nearly without exception laying down broad luminous principles, based upon reason, and those boundless stores of historical illustration, from which he argues with equal brevity and force. It is interesting to compare his treatment of the same subject in an essay and a speech. His speech on the Maynooth grant and his essay on Mr. Gladstone's *Church and State* deal with practically the same question, and few persons would hesitate to give the preference to the speech.

It is difficult to give really representative extracts from Macaulay's speeches, for the reason that they are so organically constructed that the proverbial inadequacy of the brick to represent the building applies to them in an unusual degree. Many of the speeches also refer to topics and party politics which are rapidly passing into oblivion. One subject, to our sorrow, retains a perennial interest : Macaulay's speeches on Ireland would alone

suffice to place him in the rank of high, far-seeing statesmen.   The lapse of well-nigh forty years has not aged
this melancholy retrospect.   He is speaking of Pitt's intended legislation at the time of the Union.

Unhappily, of all his projects for the benefit of Ireland, the
Union alone was carried into effect; and, therefore, that Union
was a Union only in name.   The Irish found that they had parted
with at least the name and show of independence ; and that for
this sacrifice of national pride they were to receive no compensation.   The Union, which ought to have been associated in
their minds with freedom and justice, was associated only with
disappointed hopes and forfeited pledges.   Yet it was not even
then too late.   It was not too late in 1813.   It was not too late
in 1821.   It was not too late in 1825.   Yes, if even in 1825
some men who were then as they are now, high in the service
of the Crown, could have made up their minds to do what they
were forced to do four years later, that great work of reconciliation which Mr. Pitt had meditated might have been accomplished.
The machinery of agitation was not yet fully organized.   The
Government was under no strong pressure ; and therefore
concession might still have been received with thankfulness.
That opportunity was suffered to escape, and it never returned.

In 1829, at length, concessions were made, were made
largely, were made without the conditions which Mr. Pitt
would undoubtedly have demanded, and to which, if demanded
by Mr. Pitt, the whole body of Roman Catholics would have
eagerly assented.   But those concessions were made reluctantly,
made ungraciously, made under duress, made from mere dread
of civil war.   How, then, was it possible that they should produce contentment and repose ?   What could be the effect of that
sudden and profuse liberality following that long and obstinate
resistance to the most reasonable demands, except to teach the
Irishman that he could obtain redress only by turbulence ?
Could he forget that he had been, during eight-and-twenty
years, supplicating Parliament for justice, urging those unan-
swerable arguments which prove that the rights of conscience

ought to be held sacred, claiming the performance of promises
made by ministers and princes, and that he had supplicated,
argued, claimed the performance of promises in vain? Could
he forget that two generations of the most profound thinkers,
the most brilliant wits, the most eloquent orators had written
and spoken for him in vain? Could he forget that the greatest
statesmen who took his part had paid dear for their generosity?
Mr. Pitt had endeavoured to redeem his pledge, and he was
driven from office. Lord Grey and Lord Grenville endeavoured
to do but a small part of what Mr. Pitt thought right and
expedient, and they were driven from office. Mr. Canning took
the same side, and his reward was to be worried to death by the
party of which he was the brightest ornament. At length,
when he was gone, the Roman Catholics began to look, not to
cabinets and parliaments, but to themselves. They displayed
a formidable array of physical force, and yet kept within, just
within, the limits of the law. The consequence was that,
in two years, more than any prudent friend had ventured to
demand for them was granted to them by their enemies. Yes;
within two years after Mr. Canning had been laid in the
transept near us, all that he would have done—and more than
he could have done—was done by his persecutors. How was it
possible that the whole Roman Catholic population of Ireland
should not take up the notion that, from England, or at least
from the party which then governed, and which now governs
England, nothing is to be got by reason, by entreaty, by patient
endurance, but everything by intimidation? That tardy re-
pentance deserved no gratitude, and obtained none. The whole
machinery of agitation was complete, and in perfect order.
The leaders had tasted the pleasures of popularity; the multitude had tasted the pleasures of excitement. Both the
demagogue and his audience felt a craving for the daily
stimulant. Grievances enough remained, God knows, to serve
as pretexts for agitation: and the whole conduct of the Government had led the sufferers to believe that by agitation alone
could any grievance be removed.[4]

------

[4] On the State of Ireland, Feb., 1844.

As a specimen of Macaulay's power of invective, his attack on Sir Robert Peel may be quoted. After Peel's death, when revising his speeches for publication, he recalled in his diary the impression he had made. "How white poor Peel looked while I was speaking: I remember the effect of the words, ' There you sit, &c.' "

There is too much ground for the reproaches of those who having, in spite of a bitter experience, a second time trusted the Right Honourable Baronet, now find themselves a second time deluded. It has been too much his practice, when in Opposition, to make use of passions with which he has not the slightest sympathy, and of prejudices which he regards with a profound contempt. As soon as he is in power, a change takes place. The instruments which have done his work are flung aside. The ladder by which he has climbed, is kicked down. . . . Can we wonder that the eager, honest, hot-headed Protestants, who raised you to power in the confident hope that you would curtail the privileges of the Roman Catholics, should stare and grumble when you propose to give public money to the Roman Catholics? Can we wonder that the people out of doors should be exasperated by seeing the very men who, when we were in office, voted against the old grant of Maynooth, now pushed and pulled into the House by your whippers-in to vote for an increased grant. The natural consequences follow. All those fierce spirits whom you hallooed on to harass us, now turn round and begin to worry you. The Orangeman raises his war-whoop : Exeter Hall sets up its bray: Mr. Macneill shudders to see more costly cheer than ever provided for the Priest of Baal at the table of the Queen: and the Protestant operatives of Dublin call for impeachments in exceedingly bad English. But what did you expect? Did you think when, to serve your turn, you called the devil up that it was as easy to lay him as to raise him? Did you think when you went on, session after session, thwarting and reviling those whom you knew to be in the right, and flattering all the worst passions of

those whom you knew to be in the wrong, that the day of
reckoning would never come? It has come. There you sit,
doing penance for the disingenuousness of years. If it be not
so, stand up manfully and clear your fame before the House
and country. Show us that some steady policy has guided
your conduct with respect to Irish affairs? Show us how, if
you are honest in 1845, you can have been honest in 1841?
Explain to us why, after having goaded Ireland to madness for
the purpose of ingratiating yourselves with the English, you
are now setting England on fire for the purpose of ingratiating
yourselves with the Irish? Give us some reason which shall
prove that the policy you are following, as Ministers, is entitled
to support, and which shall not equally prove you to have been
the most factious and unprincipled Opposition that ever this
country saw?" [5]

But the time was approaching when these brilliant
passages of arms needed to be brought to a close. Through
manifold impediments and hindrances, Macaulay had
slowly proceeded with his *History of England:* and he
felt what most workers have experienced, that the attractive power of his work increased with its growth. In
1844, he gave up writing for the *Edinburgh Review*, a
wise, though somewhat late resolution, which he would
have done well to make earlier. In 1847 he lost his seat
for Edinburgh, and thus was severed the last tie which
connected him with active politics. He then settled down
with steady purpose to finish his task ; and, on November
29, 1848, the work was given to the world. Not since
the publication of the first volume of the *Decline and
Fall*, nearly three-quarters of a century before, has any
historical work been received with such universal accla-
mation. The first edition of three thousand copies was
exhausted in ten days ; and in less than four months

[5] Speech on Maynooth, April, 1845.

thirteen thousand copies were sold. The way in which Macaulay was affected by this overwhelming success showed that he was wholly free from any taint of pride or arrogance. " I am half afraid," he wrote in his journal, " of this strange prosperity. . . . I feel extremely anxious about the second part. Can it possibly come up to the first ? "

We have now to consider the work in which, for many years, he had " garnered up " his heart.

CHAPTER V.

" History," says Macaulay at the commencement of the *Essay on Hallam*, " at least in its state of ideal perfection, is a compound of poetry and philosophy. It impresses general truths on the mind, by a vivid representation of particular characters and incidents. But in fact the two hostile elements of which it consists have never been known to form a perfect amalgamation ; and at length, in our own time, they have been completely and professedly separated. Good histories, in the proper sense of the word, we have not. But we have good historical romances and good historical essays."

The reconciliation of these two hostile elements of history was the dream of Macaulay's early ambition and the serious occupation of his later years. It will be worth while to briefly consider the problem itself, before we contemplate the success and skill which he brought to bear on its solution.

The two sides, or the two elements of history,—the element of fact, and the element of Art which fashions the fact into an attractive form,—have always been too obvious to be overlooked. In the earliest form of history—poetry and legend—the element of fact is reduced to a minimum, and almost completely overpowered by the element of art, which moulds fact without restraint. The growth of civic life partly redresses the balance : the need of accurate record of facts is felt, and first bald annals, and then history in the common sense of the word, make their appearance. The relative proportion of the two ingredients was never carefully determined, but left to the taste and genius of individual writers. On the whole, however, the artistic element long maintained the upper hand. The search for facts, even when acknowledged as a duty, was perfunctory, and the main object of historians was to display their talent in drawing pictures of the past, in which imagination had a larger share than reality. The masters of this artistic form of history are the four great ancients, two Greek and two Roman, Herodotus, Thucydides, Livy, and Tacitus, who have never been, and are in little danger of being, surpassed. The moderns for a long time only copied the ancients in history as in all other departments. Considering his opportunities and easy access to original authorities, Hume is hardly a more careful inquirer than Livy : an attractive narrative in a pure style was the main object of both.

But towards the end of the last century history received a new impulse. The complicated structure of society began to be dimly surmised ; political economy introduced a greater precision into the study of certain social questions; and the enlarged view thus gained of the present was soon extended to the past. The French Revolution, revealing as it did the unsuspected depth of social stratification, accelerated a movement already begun. In the early part of the present century history was studied with new eyes. It was seen that it must all be written over again—that the older writers had seen little more than the surface and were only surveyors, whereas geologists were

wanted who could penetrate to greater depths.   In short,
the past began to be scientifically examined, not for
artistic purposes in order to compose graceful narratives—
not for political purposes in order to find materials for party
warfare—not for theoretical purposes in order to construct
specious but ephemeral philosophies of history; but simply
for accurate and verifiable knowledge.   It was a repetition
of the process through which previous sciences had passed
from the pursuit of chimerical to real and valid aims—the
study of the heavens from astrology to astronomy, the
study of the constituents of bodies from alchemistry to
chemistry, the study of medicine from the search for the
elixir vitæ to serious therapeutics.   The result was to
depress, and almost degrade, the artistic element in history.
When the magnitude and severity of the task before men
was at last fully perceived—when it was seen that we have
to study the historical record as we study the geological
record—that while both are imperfect, full of gaps which
may never be filled up, yet enough remains to merit and
demand the most thorough examination, classification, and
orderly statement of the phenomena we have—it was felt
there was something trivial and unworthy of the gravity of
science to think of tricking out in the flowers of rhetoric
the hardly-won acquisitions of laborious research.   Poetical science and scientific poetry are equally repellent to
the genuine lovers of both.   Simple unornate statement
of the results obtained is the only style of treatment con-
sonant with the dignity of genuine inquiry.

Macaulay passed his youth and early manhood during
the period when this great change was taking place in
historical studies, and producing its first fruits.   But it
did not find favour in his eyes.   Very much the contrary ;
it filled him with something like disgust.   Instead of

yielding to the new movement, he resolved to ignore it, and even by his practice to oppose it. Though the two elements of history had never yet been amalgamated with success, and were about perhaps to be severed for ever, he thought he could unite them as they had never been united before. He took, as we have seen (chap. ii.), no notice of the new history, showed no curiosity in what was being done in that direction, and nursing his own thoughts in almost complete isolation amid contemporary historians, conceived and matured his own plan of how history should be written. He has left us in no doubt as to what that plan was. It was that history should be a *true novel*, capable of " interesting the affections, and presenting pictures to the imagination. . . . It should invest with the reality of human flesh and blood beings whom we are too much inclined to consider as personified qualities in an allegory ; call up our ancestors before us with all their peculiarities of language, manners, and garb ; show us over their houses, seat us at their tables, rummage their old-fashioned ward-robes, explain the uses of their ponderous furniture." And that this plan, made in youth, was carried out in after-life with rare success and felicity, his *History* is here to show. Thus, just at the time when history was taking a more scientific and impersonal character, Macaulay was pre-paring to make it more concrete and individual, to invest it with more flesh and blood, and make it more capable of stirring the affections. He was not a progressist or even a conservative, but a reactionary in his notions of history. But originality may be shown (sometimes is more shown) in going back as well as in going forward. Those are by no means the strongest minds which most readily yield to the prevailing fashion of their age. Macaulay showed a lofty self-confidence and sense of power, when he resolved to attempt a task which he owned had never been accomplished before—nay, to confer on artistic history a rank and dignity which it never had previously enjoyed, at a time when a formidable rival was threatening to depress, or even to depose it altogether.

His plan led, or rather forced him, to work on a scale of unprecedented magnitude, which, even in spite of his example, has never been quite equalled. To produce the effects he required, extreme minuteness of detail was indispensable ; characters must be painted life-size, events related with extraordinary fulness, and the history of a nation treated in a style proper to memoirs, or even to romances. The human interest had to be sustained by biographical anecdotes, and a vigilant liveliness of narrative which simulated the novel of adventure. The political interest was to be kept up by similar handling of party debates, party struggles, by one who knew by experience every inch of the ground. But the true historical and sociological interest necessarily retreated into a secondary rank. An ordnance map cannot serve the purpose of a hand atlas. On the scale of an inch to a mile we may trace the roads and boundaries of our parish ; but we cannot combine with such minuteness a synthetic view of the whole island and its relation to European geography. It was on the scale of an ordnance map that Macaulay wrote his *History of England.* Such a plan necessarily excluded as much on the one hand as it admitted on the other. Our view of the past is vitiated and wrong, unless a certain proportion presides over our conception of it. The most valuable quality of history is to show the process of social growth ; and the longer the period over which this process is observed, the more instructive is the result. A vivid perception of a short period, with imperfect grasp of what preceded and followed it, is rather misleading than instructive. It leads to a confusion of the relative importance of the part as compared to the whole.

It is perhaps a low-minded objection to Macaulay's conception of history, to remark that its application to lengthy periods is a physical impossibility. The five volumes we have of his *History* comprise a space of some fifteen years. It was his original scheme to bring his narrative down to the end of the reign of George IV., in round numbers a period of a century and a half. If therefore his plan had been carried out on its present scale, it would have needed fifty volumes, if not more, as it is highly improbable that more recent events would have permitted greater compression. But further, he wrote at an average a volume in three years ; therefore his whole task would have taken him one hundred and fifty years to accomplish—that is to say, it would have taken as long to record the events as the events took to happen. This is almost a practical refutation of the method he adopted. And yet such an absurd result could not on his principles be avoided. If history is to be written in such minute detail that it shall rival the novel in unbroken sustention of the personal interest attaching to the characters, unexampled bulk must ensue. Macaulay had no intention of being so prolix. He expected to achieve the first portion of his plan (down to the commencement of Walpole's administration), a matter of thirty-five years, in five volumes ; and as it turned out, five volumes only carried him over fifteen years. But he could not afford to reduce his scale without sacrificing his conception of how history should be written.

What was the new and original element in Macaulay's treatment of history ? The unanimous verdict of his

contemporaries was to the effect that he *had* treated
history in a novel way.   He was himself satisfied that he
had improved on his predecessors.   " There is merit, no
doubt," he says, in his diary, "in Hume, Robertson,
Voltaire, and Gibbon.   Yet it is not the thing.   I have
a conception of history more just, I am confident, than
theirs."   Self-conceit was no vice of Macaulay's; and as on
this point of his originality he persuaded all the reading
world of his time to adopt his opinion, our business is to
find out in what his originality consisted.   What it amounts
to, or may be intrinsically worth, will be considered afterwards.

If we take to pieces one of his massive chapters with
a view to examine his method, we shall find that his self-
confidence was not without foundation.   Historical narrative in his hands is something vastly more complex and
involved than it ever was before.   Indeed " narrative "
is a weak and improper word to express the highly
organized structure of his composition.   Beneath the
smooth and polished surface layer under layer may be
seen of subordinate narratives, crossing and interlacing
each other like the parts in the score of an oratorio.   And
this complexity results not in confusion, but in the most
admirable clearness and unity of effect.   His pages are
not only pictorial, they are dramatic.   Scene is made to
follow scene with the skill of an accomplished playwright;
and each has been planned and fashioned with a view to
its thoughtfully prepared place in the whole piece.   The
interest of the story as a story is kept up with a profound
and unsuspected art.   The thread of the narrative is never
dropped.   When transitions occur—and no writer passes
from one part of his subject to another with more boldness
and freedom—they are managed with such skill and ease

that the reader is unaware of them. A turn of the road has brought us in view of a new prospect; but we are not conscious for a moment of having left the road. The change seems the most natural thing in the world. Let the more remarkable chapters be examined from this point of view—say, simply for example, the Ninth, the Fifteenth, and the Twentieth—and then let the most adverse critic be asked to name an instance in which the art of historical composition has been carried to a higher perfection.

In short, Macaulay was a master of the great art of *mise-en-scène*, such as we never had before. It is rather a French than an English quality, and has been duly appreciated in France. Michelet praises Macaulay in warm terms, speaks of him as "*illustre et regretté*," and of his "*très beau récit.*" If he must be considered as an historical artist who on the whole has no equal, the fact is not entirely owing to the superiority of his genius, unmistakable as that was. No historian before him ever regarded his task from the same point of view, or aimed with such calm patience and labour at the same result; no one, in short, had ever so resolved to treat real events on the lines of the novel or romance. Many writers before Macaulay had done their best to be graphic and picturesque, but none ever saw that the scattered fragments of truth could, by incessant toil directed by an artistic eye, be worked into a mosaic, which for colour, freedom, and finish, might rival the creations of fancy. The poets who have written history—Voltaire, Southey, Schiller, Lamartine—are not comparable to Macaulay as historical artists. They did not see that facts recorded in old books, if collected and sorted with unwearied pains, might be made to produce effects nearly as striking and brilliant as the facts they invented for the works of

L

their imagination. Macaulay saw that the repertory of
truth was hardly less extensive than the repertory of
fiction. If the biography of every character is known
with the utmost detail, it will be possible, when each
presents himself in the narrative, to introduce him with a
fulness of portraiture such as the novelist applies to the
hero and heroine of his romance. Exhaustive knowledge
of the preceding history of every place named, enables
the writer to sketch the castle, the town, or the manor
house with opportune minuteness and local colour. Above
all, a narrative built on so large a scale that it allows
absolutely unlimited copiousness of facts and illustration,
can be ordered with that regard to the interest of the
story as a story that the universal curiosity in human
adventure is awakened which produces the constant
demand for works of fiction. Macaulay saw this, and
carried out his conception with a genius and patient
diligence which, when our attention is fully called to the
point, fill the mind with something like amazement. It
is probable that no historian ever devoted such care to
the grouping of his materials.   He re-planned and re-wrote
whole chapters with ungrudging toil. " I worked hard,"
he says, in his diary, " at altering the arrangement of the
first three chapters of the third volume.   What labour it
is to make a tolerable book ; and how little readers know
how much trouble the ordering of parts has cost the writer."
Again : " This is a tough chapter. To make the narrative
flow along as it ought, each part naturally springing from
that which precedes, is not easy. What trouble these
few pages have cost me. The great object is that they
may read as if they had been spoken off, and seem to flow
as easily as table-talk." Any one who knows by experience
how difficult it is to conduct a wide complex narrative

with perspicuity and ease, and then observes the success
with which Macaulay has conquered the difficulty, will
be apt to fall into a mute admiration almost too deep for
praise. In the "ordering of parts," which cost him so
much labour, his equal will not easily be found. Each
side of the story is brought forward in its proper time
and place, and leaves the stage when it has served its
purpose, that of advancing by one step the main action.
Each of these subordinate stories, marked by exquisite
finish, leads up to a minor crisis or turn in events, where
it joins the chief narrative with a certain *éclat* and
surprise. The interweaving of these well-nigh endless
threads, the clearness with which each is kept visible and
distinct, and yet is made to contribute its peculiar effect
and colour to the whole texture, constitute one of the
great feats in literature.

Imperfectly as a notion of such constant and pervading
merit can be conveyed by an extract, one is offered here
merely as an example. But a passage from Hume, dealing
with the same events, will be given first. An interesting
comparison—or rather, contrast—between the styles of the
earlier and later writer will be found to result. The
subject is the flight of the Princess Anne at the crisis of
her father's fortunes. Hume says :—

But Churchill had prepared a still more mortal blow for his
distressed benefactor. His lady and he had an entire ascendant
over the family of Prince George of Danemark ; and the time
now appeared seasonable for overwhelming the unhappy king,
who was already staggering with the violent shocks which he
had received. Andover was the first stage of James's retreat
towards London, and there Prince George, together with the
young Duke of Ormond, Sir George Huet, and some other persons of distinction, deserted him in the night time, and retired

to the Prince's camp. No sooner had this news reached London,
than the Princess Anne, pretending fear of the king's displeasure,
withdrew herself in company with the bishop of London and
Lady Churchill. She fled to Nottingham, where the Earl of
Dorset received her with great respect, and the gentry of the
country quickly formed a troop for her protection.

This is Macaulay's account :—

Prince George, and Ormond, were invited to sup with the
king at Andover. The meal must have been a sad one. The
king was overwhelmed by his misfortunes. His son-in-law was
the dullest of companions. " I have tried Prince George sober,"
said Charles the Second, " and I have tried him drunk ; and
drunk or sober, there is nothing in him." Ormond, who was
through life taciturn and bashful, was not likely to be in high
spirits at such a moment. At length the repast terminated. The
king retired to rest. Horses were in waiting for the Prince and
Ormond, who, as soon as they left the table, mounted and
rode off. They were accompanied by the Earl of Drumlanrig,
eldest son of the Duke of Queensberry. The defection of this
young nobleman was no insignificant event. For Queensberry
was the head of the Protestant episcopalians of Scotland, a class
compared with whom the bitterest English Tories might be called
Whiggish ; and Drumlanrig himself was lieutenant-colonel of
Dundee's regiment of horse, a band more detested by the Whigs
then even Kirke's lambs. This fresh calamity was announced to
the king on the following morning. He was less disturbed
by the news than might have been expected. The shock which
he had undergone twenty-four hours before had prepared him
for almost any disaster ; and it was impossible to be seriously
angry with Prince George, who was hardly an accountable being,
for having yielded to the arts of such a tempter as Churchill.
" What ! " said James, " Is Est-il-possible gone too ? After all,
a good trooper would have been a greater loss." In truth the
king's whole anger seems at this time to have been concentrated, and not without cause, on one object. He set off for

London, breathing vengeance against Churchill, and learned on
arriving a new crime of the arch-deceiver. The Princess Anne
had been some hours missing.

Observe the art with which the flight of the princess
has been kept back, till it can be revealed with startling
effect.   The humorous story continues. —

Anne, who had no will but that of the Churchills, had been
induced by them to notify under her own hand to William, a
week before, her approbation of his enterprise. She assured him
that she was entirely in the hands of her friends, and that she
would remain in the palace or take refuge in the city as they
might determine.   On Sunday, 25th November, she and those
who thought for her were under the necessity of coming to a
sudden resolution.   That afternoon a courier from Salisbury
brought tidings that Churchill had disappeared, and that he had
been accompanied by Grafton, that Kirke had proved false, and
that the royal forces were in full retreat.   There was, as usually
happened when great news, good or bad, arrived in town, an
immense crowd that evening in the gallery of Whitehall.
Curiosity and anxiety sate on every face.   The Queen broke
forth into natural expressions of indignation against the chief
traitor, and did not altogether spare his too partial mistress.
The sentinels were doubled round that part of the palace which
Anne occupied.   The princess was in dismay.   In a few hours
her father would be at Westminster.   It was not likely that he
would treat her personally with severity; but that he would
permit her any longer to enjoy the society of her friend was not
to be hoped.   It could hardly be doubted that Sarah would be
placed under arrest, and would be subjected to a strict examination by shrewd and rigorous inquisitors.   Her papers would be
seized; perhaps evidence affecting her life would be discovered;
if so, the worst might well be dreaded.   The vengeance of the
implacable king knew no distinction of sex.   For offences much
smaller than those which might be brought home to Lady
Churchill, he had sent women to the scaffold and the stake.

Strong affection braced the feeble mind of the princess. There was no tie which she would not break, no risk which she would not run, for the object of her idolatrous affection. "I will jump out of the window," she cried, "rather than be found here by my father." The favourite undertook to manage an escape. She communicated in all haste with some of the chiefs of the conspiracy. In a few hours everything was arranged. That evening Anne retired to her chamber as usual. At dead of night she rose, and accompanied by her friend Sarah and two other female attendants, stole down the back stairs in a dressing-gown and slippers. The fugitive gained the open street un-challenged. A hackney coach was in waiting for them there. Two men guarded the humble vehicle; one of them was Comp-ton, Bishop of London, the princess's old tutor; the other was the magnificent and accomplished Dorset, whom the extremity of the public danger had aroused from his luxurious repose. The coach drove to Aldersgate Street, where the town residence of the Bishops of London then stood, within the shadow of their cathedral. There the princess passed the night. On the fol-lowing morning she set out for Epping Forest. In that wild tract Dorset possessed a venerable mansion, which has long since been destroyed. In his hospitable dwelling, the favourite resort of wits and poets, the fugitives made a short stay. They could not safely attempt to reach William's quarters, for the road thither lay through a country occupied by the royal forces. It was therefore determined that Anne should take refuge with the northern insurgents. Compton wholly laid aside for the time his sacerdotal character. Danger and conflict had rekindled in him all the military ardour which he had felt twenty-eight years before, when he rode in the Life Guards. He preceded the princess's carriage in a buff coat and jackboots, with a sword at his side, and pistols in his holsters. Long before she reached Nottingham she was surrounded by a body-guard of gentlemen who volunteered to escort her. They invited the bishop to act as their colonel, and he assented with an alacrity which gave great scandal to rigid churchmen, and did not much raise his character even in the opinion of Whigs.

Reserving the question whether history gains or loses by being written in this way—a most important reservation—it must be allowed that of its kind this is nearly as good as it can be. The sprightly vivacity of the scene is worthy of any novel, yet it is all a mosaic of actual fact. We may call it Richardson grafted on Hume.

Passages like these, as every reader knows, are incessant in Macaulay's *History*, and have been the foundation of a common charge of " excess of ornament." In this there seems to be some misconception, or even confusion of mind, on the part of those who bring the accusation. It is obviously open to us to object to this mode of treating history altogether. We may say that to recount the history of a great state in a sensational style befitting the novel of adventure is a mistaken proceeding. But this objection eliminates Macaulay's *History* from the pale of toleration. According to his scheme such passages are not mere ornament, but part and parcel of the whole structure ; to remove them would not be to remove mere excrescences, but a large portion of the substance as well. We must make our choice between two styles of history —the one in which the interest centres round human characters, and the other in which it centres round the growth and play of social forces. Perhaps the two may very well exist side by side—perhaps not ; but in any case we cannot with fairness employ the principles of the one to criticize the methods of the other. Macaulay wittingly, and after mature thought, adopted the style we know, and carried it out with a sumptuous pomp that has never been surpassed. His ornament, it will be generally found, is no idle embellishment, stuck on with vulgar profusion in obedience to a faulty taste, but structurally useful parts of the building, supporting, according to size and position, a due share of the weight ; or, in other words, mere additional facts for which he is able to find a fitting place. Take, for instance, this little vignette of Monmouth and the Princess of Orange :—

The duke had been encouraged to hope that in a very short time he would be recalled to his native land and restored to all his high honours and commands. Animated by such expectations, he had been the life of the Hague during the late winter. He had been the most conspicuous figure at a succession of balls in that splendid Orange hall which blazes on every side with the most ostentatious colouring of Jordaens and Hondthorst. He had taught the English country-dance to the Dutch ladies, and had in his turn learned from them to skate on the canals. The princess had accompanied him in his expeditions on the ice ; and the figure which she made there, poised on one leg, and clad in petticoats shorter than are generally worn by ladies so strictly decorous, had caused some wonder and mirth to the foreign ministers. The sullen gravity which had been characteristic of the Stadtholder's court, seemed to have vanished before the influence of the fascinating Englishman. Even the stern and pensive William relaxed into good-humour when his brilliant guest appeared.

Will any one say that this is idle and redundant ornament ? Could the two men who came to deliver England from the dull folly of James II. be more clearly and rapidly sketched, and the failure of the one and the success of the other more suggestively traced back to the difference of their respective characters ?

A similar remark applies to the careful and elaborate portraits by which all the chief and most of the secondary characters are introduced. They have been much blamed —and with reason—by those whose notions of history are opposed to Macaulay's. It must be admitted also that he had not a quick eye for character, and little of that skill which sketches in a few strokes the memorable features of a face or a mind. Still from his point of view such portraits were quite legitimate, and it cannot be denied that in their way they are often admirably done. They overflow with knowledge, they convey it in an attractive form, and they are inserted with great art just when they are wanted. Even their length, which sometimes must be pronounced excessive, never seems to interfere with the action of the story. In such an extensive gallery it is difficult to make a selection. Perhaps the Twentieth chapter, containing the fine series of portraits of Sunderland, Russell, Somers, Montague, Wharton, and Harley, may be named as among the most remarkable. Taken altogether they occupy more than twenty pages. An important subject—the first formation of a Ministry in the modern sense of the word—is dropped for the purpose of introducing them, yet so skilful is the handling that we are conscious of no confusing interruption. This merit distinguishes Macaulay's illustrations, and even digressions, almost invariably. They never seem to be digressions. Instead of quenching the interest they heighten it; and after his widest excursions he brings the reader back to the original point with a curiosity more keen than ever in the main story. Greater evidence of power could hardly be given.

In criticizing Macaulay's *History* we should ever bear in mind it is after all only a fragment, though a colossal fragment. We have only a small portion of the edifice that he had planned in his mind. History, which has so many points of contact with architecture, resembles it also in this, that in both impressiveness largely depends on size. A few arches can give no adequate notion of the long

colonnade. Of Macaulay's work we have, so to speak,
only a few arches. It is true that he built on such a
scale that the full completion of his design was beyond
the limited span of one man's life and power. But had
he lived ten or fifteen years longer—as he well might,
and then not have exceeded the age of several of his great
contemporaries, Hallam, Thiers, Guizot, Michelet, Ranke,
Carlyle—and carried on his work to double or treble its
present length, it is difficult to exaggerate the increased
grandeur which would have resulted. Such a structure,
so spacious and lofty, required length for harmonious proportion. As it is, the *History of England* reminds one of
the unfinished cathedral of Beauvais. The ornate and
soaring choir wants the balance of a majestic nave, and
the masterpiece of French Gothic is deprived of its proper
rank from mere incompleteness.

Unfortunately the *History* can be reproached with more
serious faults than incompleteness. The most common
objections are the unfair party-spirit supposed to pervade
the book, and its strange inaccuracies as to matters of
fact.

The accusation of party-spirit seems on the whole to be
unfounded, and we may suspect is chiefly made by those
whose own prejudices are so strong that they resent impartiality nearly as much as hostility. He that is not
with them is against them. Macaulay when he wrote
his *History*, had ceased to be a party man as regards contemporary politics, and in his work he is neither a Whig
nor a Tory but a Williamite. He over and over condemns
the Whigs in unqualified terms, and he always does
justice to the really upright and high-minded Tories. The
proof of this will be found in the warmth of his eulogy
and admiration for eminent nonjurors, such as Bishop Ken

and Jeremy Collier. As clergymen and uncompromising Tories they would have been equally repugnant to him, if party-spirit had governed his sympathies to the extent supposed. The fact is that there are few characters mentioned in the whole course of his *History* of whom he speaks in such warm, almost such enthusiastic, praise. Of the sainted Bishop of Wells he writes with a reverence which is not a common sentiment with him for anybody. Of the author of a *Short View of the English Stage*, he is likely to be thought by those who have read that book to speak with excessive eulogy. But he considered them very justly to be thoroughly upright and conscientious men, and for such it must be admitted he had a very partial feeling. It would not be easy to show that he has ever been unjust or at all unfair to the Tories as a party or as individuals. He blames them freely; but so he blames the Whigs. The real origin of this charge of party-spirit may probably be traced to the unfavourable impression he conveys of the house of Stuart. The sentimental Jacobitism fostered by Scott and others, took offence at his treatment of the king of the cavaliers and his two sons. But is he unfair, or even unduly severe? If ever a dynasty of princes was condemned, and deserved condemnation, at the bar of history, it was that perverse and incompetent race, who plotted and carried out their own destruction with a perseverance which other sovereigns have brought to the consolidation of their power. Are impartial foreigners, such as Ranke and Gneist, less severe? On the contrary. "Another royal family," says the latter, " could hardly be named which has shown on the throne in an equal degree such a total want of all sense of kingly duty." Nay, we have what some persons will consider the highest authority pronouncing in Macaulay's favour. We read in his diary of March 9, 1850 : "To dinner at the palace. The Queen was most gracious to me. She talked much about my book, and owned she had nothing to say for her poor ancestor James II." One can understand a preference for arbitrary power ; one can appreciate an admiration for the heroic Strafford. But Charles I. and James II. were mere blunderers, whose lust for power was only equalled by their inability to use it.

With regard to individuals the case is different. He allowed himself to cultivate strong antipathies towards a number of persons— statesmen, soldiers, men of letters— in the past, and he pursued them with a personal animosity which could hardly have been exceeded if they had crossed him in the club or the House of Commons. He conceived a contemptuous view of their characters ; his strong historical imagination gave them the reality of living beings, whom he was always meeting "in the corridors of Time," and each encounter embittered his hostility. Marlborough, Penn, and Dundee (in his *History*), Boswell, Impey, and Walpole (in his *Essays*), always more or less stir his bile, and his prejudice leads him into serious inaccuracies. One naturally seeks to inquire what may have been the cause of such obliquity in a man who was never, by enmity itself, accused of wanting generous feelings, and whom it is almost impossible to suspect of conscious unfairness. The truth seems to be that Macaulay had, like most eminent men, *les défauts de ses qualités.* One of his qualities was a punctilious regard for truth and straightforward dealing. Another was supreme common sense. The first made him hate and despise knaves, the second made him detest dunces ; and he did both with unnecessary scorn—with a sort of donnish and self-righteous complacency which is anything but winning. He made up his mind that Boswell was a pushing impertinent fool ; and for fools he had no mercy. He satisfied himself that Bacon was a corrupt judge ; that Impey was an unjust judge ; that Marlborough was a base, avaricious time-server ; and that Penn was a pompous hypocrite, or something very like it. For such vices he had little or no tolerance, and he was somewhat inclined to lose his head in his anger at them. That in all the cases referred to, he showed precipitancy, and what is worse, obstinate persistence in error, unfortunately cannot be denied. But there was nothing unworthy in his primary impulse. It was a perverted form of the sense of justice to which upright men are sometimes prone, somewhat resembling that arrogance of virtue which misleads good women into harshness towards their less immaculate sisters.

Whatever this plea may be worth, it cannot blind us to the serious breaches of historical fidelity which he has been led to commit. Mr. Paget, in his *New Examen*, has proved beyond question that, with regard to Marlborough and Penn, Macaulay has been guilty of gross inaccuracy, nay, even perversions of the truth. For details of the evidence, the reader must consult Mr. Paget. The miscarriage of the attack on Brest, which Macaulay lays exclusively " on the basest of all the hundred villanies of Marlborough," is shown to have failed through the imprudent valour of Talmash. William and his ministers were well aware that the French knew of the expedition, and had long been prepared to repel it. The king writes, "They were long apprised of our intended attack ;" and mildly lays the blame on the rashness of his own general. But Macaulay makes it appear that through Marlborough's treachery the English forces went blindly to their own destruction. Expecting to surprise the French,

we are told they found them armed to the teeth, solely in
consequence of information sent to James II. by Churchill;
hence the failure, and the deaths of Talmash and many
brave men, of whom Macaulay does not scruple to call
Marlborough the "murderer." It must be owned that
this is very serious : and it does not much mend the
matter to ascribe, as we surely may, Macaulay's inaccuracy
to invincible prejudice, rather than to ignorance or dis-
honesty. He was thoroughly convinced that Marlborough
was a faithless intriguer, which may be quite true ; but
that was no reason for charging him with crimes which he
did not commit. Let it be noticed, however, that the
refusal to be dazzled by military glory, and to accept it as
a set off to any moral delinquency, is no vulgar merit in
an historian. Mr. Carlyle has been heard to say that
Rhadamanthus would certainly give Macaulay four dozen
lashes when he went to the Shades, for his treatment of
Marlborough. This is quite in character for the Scotch
apostle of "blood and iron." Macaulay could admire
military genius when united with magnanimity and public
virtue as warmly as any one. But he could not accept it
as a compensation for the want of truth and honour.

His treatment of Penn admits of the same kind of
imperfect palliation. He had satisfied himself that the
Quaker was, for a time at least, a time-server and a syco-
phant. And he allowed his disgust at such a character
to hurry him into culpable unfairness, which has been
exposed by the late Mr. Hepworth Dixon, and Mr. W. E.
Forster, as well as by Mr. Paget. The animosity
with which he pursues Penn—the false colouring
amounting, in places, to real misrepresentation, which
he gives to actions innocent or laudable, can only excite
astonishment and regret. His account of Penn's inter-

ference in the dispute between the king and Magdalen
College is almost mendacious.   He would make it appear
that Penn acted merely as a ready and unscrupulous tool
of James II.   "The courtly Quaker did his best to seduce
the College from the right path.   He first tried intimidation." (*Hist.* cap. viii.)   Now nothing is more certain than
that it was the College which invoked Penn's mediation
with the king.   The whole subject is a painful one, and
we would gladly leave it.   The only inducement we can
have to linger over it is the query What was the chief
motive or origin of such historical unfaithfulness ?   A
partial answer to this question has been attempted above,
—that a wrong-headed species of righteous indignation
got possession of the writer's mind, and led him into the
evil paths of injustice and untruth.   But there was besides
another temptation to lead Macaulay astray, to which few
historians have been exposed in an equal degree.   His
plan of assimilating real to fictitious narrative—of writing
history on the lines of the novel—obscured or confused
his vision for plain fact.   His need of lighter and darker
shades caused him to make colours when he could not
find them ; his necessities as an artist forced him to
correct the adverse fortune which had not provided him
with the tints which his purpose required.   No well-
constructed play or novel can dispense with a villain
whose vices throw up in brighter relief the virtues of the
hero and heroine.   That he did yield to this temptation,
we have ample evidence.   It caused him to use his
authorities in a way that serious history must entirely
condemn.   Mr. Spedding has shown how freely he
deviated into fiction in his libel on Bacon : a molecule
of truth serves as a basis for a superstructure of fancy.
To Bacon's intellectual greatness a contrast was needed—

and it is found partly in the generosity of Essex, and
partly in his own supposed moral baseness. A good
instance of Macaulay's tendency to pervert his authorities
to artistic uses, will be found in his account of the dying
speech of Robert Francis, who was executed for the alleged
murder of Dangerfield, by striking him in the eye with a
cane. Repelling a scandalous report that the act had been
prompted by jealousy, on the ground of Dangerfield's
criminal relations with his wife, Francis declared on the
scaffold that he was certain that she had never seen him
in her whole life, and added, " besides that, she is as
virtuous a woman as lives ; and born of so good and loyal
a family, she would have scorned to prostitute herself to
such a profligate person." In Macaulay's version this
statement is altered and dressed up thus :—

> The dying husband, with an earnestness half ridiculous half
> pathetic, vindicated the lady's character ; she was, he said, a vir-
> tuous woman, she came of a loyal stock, and if she had been
> inclined to break her marriage vow, would at least have selected
> a Tory and a churchman for her paramour.

This is the result of treating history in the style of
romance. It is, no doubt, probably true, that if the
virtuous and calumniated Mrs. Francis had permitted
herself to have a paramour, he would have been a Tory
and a churchman. But what are we to think of an
historian who presents in *oratio obliqua* this poetic probability as the actual assertion of the dying husband ?

It is even less easy to account for Macaulay's treatment
of the Anglican clergy. No one thing in his *History* gave
such deep and permanent offence. It is difficult even
to surmise a reason for the line he took. The imperfect
excuses which may be pleaded for his injustice to indivi-

duals, will not avail in this case. Neither an ill-regulated zeal for virtue, nor the needs of picturesque history, demanded the singular form of depreciation of the English clergy which he has allowed himself. He does not arraign their morality, or their patriotism, or even their culture on the whole—but their social position : they were not gentlemen ; they were regarded as on the whole a plebeian class ; "for one who made the figure of a gentleman, ten were menial servants." He must have been well aware that such a reflection conveyed an affront which in our society would not readily be forgiven. Nor has it been. One frequently meets with persons who will not tolerate a good word for Macaulay ; and if the ground of their repugnance is sought for, we generally find it in these remarks upon the clergy. The climax of insult was reached in the aspersion thrown on the wives of clergy-men, that they were generally women whose " characters had been blown upon ;" and this is based on no better authority than a line in Swift—unusually audacious, cynical, and indecent, even for him. The tone of the whole passage—some eight or ten pages—savours more of satire and caricature than of sober history. Whether that " invincible suspicion of parsons " which Mr. Leslie Stephen declares to be a characteristic of the true Whig, was at the bottom of it, one would not like to say. But few would deny that Macaulay, in his treatment of the Church of England has more openly yielded to the promptings of party-spirit than any in other portions of his *History*.

Nevertheless, they deceive themselves who think that they can brand Macaulay with the stigma of habitual and pervading unfaithfulness. He does not belong to that select band of writers whose accuracy may be taken

for granted—to the class of Bentley, Gibbon, and Bayle—
who seem provided with an extra sense which saves them
from the shortcomings of other men.   He has a share of
ordinary human infirmity, but not a large share.   He can
be prejudiced and incorrect ; but these failings are most
assuredly the exception, not the rule.   Above all, he
impresses all impartial judges with a conviction of his
honesty.   "There never was a writer less capable of
intentional unfairness," says Mr. Gladstone, who still is
well aware how inaccurate he could be on occasion.   His
inaccuracy arose from hearty dislike for men of whom he
honestly thought ill.   Of conscious duplicity and untruth,
no one who knows him can conceive him guilty.

We now turn to the reservation made a few pages
back, and inquire how far Macaulay's conception of
history deserves to be commended in itself, irrespective of
the talent with which he put it into execution.

In a letter to Macvey Napier, Macaulay wrote : "I
have at last begun my historical labours. . . . . The
materials for an amusing narrative are immense.   I shall
not be satisfied unless I produce something which shall
for a few days supersede the last fashionable novel on the
tables of young ladies."   We did not need this intimation
to make us acquainted with the chief object which the
writer had in view ; but it is satisfactory to have it, as
now no doubt remains on the subject.   This, then, was
Macaulay's pole-star, by which he guided his historical
argosy over the waters of the past—young ladies for
readers, laying down the novel of the season to take up his
History of England.   His star led him to the port for which
he steered.   But how widely it made him depart from the
great ocean highway frequented by ships bound for more
daring ventures, it is now our business to examine and show.

The chief objections which may be made against the *History* are the following :—

(1.) Want of generalized and synthetic views.

(2.) Excessive diffuseness.

(3.) Deficient historical spirit.

(1.) As a work of art the *History* is so bright and impressive, it appeals so strongly to the imagination, that we do not at first perceive how little it appeals to the reason, or how little it offers by way of enlightenment to the mind. Any page, or even chapter taken at random, is almost sure to charm us by its colour, variety, and interest. But when we read a whole volume, or still more the whole work through, pretty rapidly, we become conscious of a great omission. In spite of the amazing skill of the narrative, of the vivid and exciting scenes that are marshalled past us as on some great stage, the reflective faculty finds its interest diminishing ; while the eye and the fancy are surfeited with good things, the intellect is sent empty away. It is not easy to retain any definite impression of what the book has taught us. We remember that while reading it we had a most amusing entertainment, that crowds of people in old-fashioned costumes who took part in exciting scenes were presented us. But our recollection of the whole resembles very much our recollection of a carnival or a masqued ball a few weeks after it is over. Our memory of English history seems to have been at once brightened and confused.

The reason, as Macaulay would have said, is very obvious: while no historian ever surpassed him in the art of brilliantly narrating events, few among the men of mark have been so careless or incapable of classifying them in luminous order which attracts the attention of the mind. Engrossed with the dramatic and pictorial side of history, he paid little attention to that side which gives expression to general views, which embraces a mass of details in an abstract statement, thereby throwing vastly increased light and interest on the details themselves. He never resumes in large traits the character of an epoch—never traces in clear outline the movement (entwicklungsgang) of a period, showing as on a skeleton map the line of progress. It does not appear that he yielded to the silly notion that abstract history must necessarily be incorrect. All history unfortunately is liable to be incorrect, and concrete history as much as any. It is nearly as easy to blunder in summing up the character of a man—as Penn or Marlborough—as in summing up the character of a period. There can be no doubt, however, which is the more valuable and important thing to do. History must become a chaos, if its increasing volume and complexity are not lightened and methodized by general and synthetic views. It is in this respect that the modern school of history is so superior to the ancient. We may see this by remarking the errors into which the greatest men formerly fell, from which very small men are now preserved. When we find such a statesman as Machiavelli ascribing the fall of the Roman Empire to the treachery and ambition of Stilicho, who "contrived that the Burgundians, Franks, Vandals, and Alans should assail the Roman provinces;" when we find such a genius as Montesquieu accounting for the same catastrophe by the imprudent transfer of the seat of empire, which carried all the wealth from Rome to Constantinople ; or such a scholar as Gibbon still explaining the same event by the refusal of the Roman legionaries to wear defensive armour, we are able to appreciate the progress that has been made in comprehending the past. Those great men saw nothing absurd in at-

tributing the most momentous social transformation
recorded in history to quite trivial and superficial causes.
If we know better, it is because the study of society,
whether past or present, has made some progress towards
scientific shape.   This progress was not furthered by
Macaulay.   He contributed nothing to our intelligence of
the past, though he did so much for its pictorial illustration.

For instance.   He has not grasped and reproduced in
well-weighed general proportions the import and historical
meaning of the Stuart period, which was his real object.
He has painted many phases of it with almost redundant
fulness.   But he has not traced the evolution of those
ideas and principles which mark its peculiar character.
He mentions the "strange theories of Filmer," but instead
of pointing out their origin, and the causes of their growth
(which was the historical problem) he seriously controverts
them from the modern point of view, as if Filmer needed
refuting now-a-days.   He devotes over two pages to this
work of supererogation.   But if we ask why this notion
of divine right rose into such prominence at this particular
time, he has nothing to say.   He rarely or never *accounts*
for a phase of thought, institution, or line of policy,
tracing it back to antecedent causes, and showing how
under the circumstances it was the natural and legitimate
result.   What he does is to *describe* it with often wearisome prolixity.   He describes the Church of England over
and over again from the outside, from a sort of dissenter's
point of view; but except the not recondite suggestion
that the Church of England was a compromise between
the "Church of Rome and the Church of Geneva," he
really tells us nothing.   This idea of a compromise strikes
him as so weighty and important that he develops it with

an elaboration which is common with him, and which Mr.
Leslie Stephen irreverently calls his zeal "for blacking
the chimney." Thus :—

In every point of her system the same policy may be traced.
Utterly rejecting the doctrine of transubstantiation, and condemning as idolatrous all adoration paid to sacramental bread and
wine, she yet, to the disgust of the Puritan, required her children
to receive the memorials of Divine love meekly kneeling upon
their knees. Discarding many rich vestments which surrounded
the altars of the ancient faith, she yet retained, to the horror of
weak minds, the robe of white linen, which typified the purity
which belonged to her as the mystical spouse of Christ. Discarding a crowd of pantomimic gestures, which in the Roman
Catholic worship are substituted for intelligible words, she yet
shocked many rigid Protestants by marking the infant just
sprinkled from the font, with the sign of the cross. The Roman
Catholic addressed his prayers to a multitude of saints, among
whom were numbered many men of doubtful, and some of hateful character. The Puritan refused the addition of saint, even
to the Apostle of the Gentiles and to the disciple whom Jesus
loved. The Church of England, though she asked for the inter-
cession of no created being, still set apart days for the commemo-
ration of some who had done and suffered great things for the
faith. She retained confirmation and ordination, as edifying
rites, but she degraded them from the rank of sacraments.
Shrift was no part of her system; yet she gently invited the
dying penitent to confess his sins to a divine, and empowered
her ministers to soothe the departing soul by an absolution which
breathes the very spirit of the old religion. In general, it may
be said that she appeals more to the understanding, and less to
the senses and the imagination, than the Church of Rome; and
that she appeals less to the understanding, and more to the senses
and imagination, than the Protestant churches of Scotland, France,
and Switzerland.

There are five pages more of a quality quite up to this

sample.   Now the point to be noticed is that this is not
history at all.   The historian of the seventeenth century
is not concerned with what the Church of England is or
is not ; *but with how she came to be what she was in the
days of the Stuarts.*   What we want to know is how and
why the Puritan bishops of Elizabeth were succeeded in
a few years by the High Church bishops of James and
Charles.   Those who ask these questions must not address
themselves to Macaulay.   He can only tell them that " the
Arminian doctrine spread fast and wide," and that "the
infection soon reached the court."   Why the transformation of opinion took place he does not attempt to explain.
The singular theory which he held as to the inherent un-
reasonableness of *all* religious opinion, that it was a matter
of mere accident and caprice, no doubt seriously hampered
him in his treatment of these topics.   But it is strange
that he was not surprised at his own inability to deal with
a whole order of historical phenomena of constant recur-
rence since Europe became Christian.   How differently
did Gibbon handle a vastly more difficult theme—the
orthodox and heretical dogmas of the early Church.

Even the constitutional side of his subject is neglected,
though probably few historians or politicians have known it
better or have valued it more.   But we look in vain in his
pages for a clear exposition, freed from the confusion of
details, of the progressive stages of the conflict between the
crown and the parliament during the Stuart period—the *mo-
menta* of the struggle set forth in luminous order, showing
how a move on one side was answered by a move on the
other.   In vivid concrete narrative Macaulay has few equals ;
but in that form of abstract narrative which traces the central idea and energy of a social movement, carefully exclud-
ing the disturbing intrusion of particular facts, he showed

little aptitude ; when he attempts it, he cannot maintain it for long ; he falls off into his bright picturesque style. It is not easy to see what purpose Macaulay had in view by writing his first chapter in its present form. A brief and weighty sketch of the growth and progress of the English constitution would have been a worthy preface to his history of the last great struggle for parliamentary government. But he has not attempted anything of the kind. It would not have occurred to every one to review English history from the Saxon times, and not mention once Simon de Montfort's name, nor even refer to the institutions he fostered, except with a vagueness that was utterly unmeaning. The thirteenth century he describes as a " sterile and obscure " portion of our annals. He even does his best to appear guilty of an ignorance with which it is impossible to credit him. Speaking of the Norman Conquest, he says " the talents and even the virtues of the first six French kings were a curse to England ; the follies and vices of the seventh were her salvation." And why ? Because " If John had inherited the great qualities of his father, of Henry Beauclerc, or of the Conqueror . . . . the house of Plantagenet must have risen to unrivalled ascendency in Europe." Frightful results would have followed. " England would never have had an independent existence . . . . the noble language of Milton and Burke would have remained a rustic dialect, without a literature, a fixed grammar, or a fixed orthography." It is not easy to believe that Macaulay was unaware of the debt that England owed to her vigorous Norman and Angevin kings—that their strong despotism carried our country rapidly through several stages of political development, for which other nations had to wait for centuries. In the same light vein he has a strange paragraph about the " parliamentary assem-

blies " of Europe, in which he contrasts the failure of
parliamentary government on the Continent with its
success in England. The reason was that those assemblies
were not wise like the English parliament was, they were
not sufficiently vigilant and cautious in voting taxes. The
policy which they " ought to have adopted was to take
their stand firmly on their constitutional right to give or
withhold money, and resolutely to refuse funds for the
support of armies, till ample securities had been provided
against despotism. This wise policy was followed in our
country alone." This policy succeeded in England alone ;
but it was tried repeatedly in France and Spain during
several centuries, and if it failed it was certainly not
because Frenchmen and Spaniards overlooked its wisdom,
but because that unanimity of national life which the
Norman Conquest had produced in England was absent in
those countries. But Macaulay as an historian cared for
none of these things. His morbid dread of dulness made
him shrink from them. In this very chapter, where he
cannot find space for the most important topics of English
history, he readily dilates in his picturesque way on the
manners of the Normans during a page and a half.

(2.) As regards his diffuseness there can be but one
opinion. The way in which he will go on repeating the
same idea in every form and variation that his vast
resources of language enabled him to command, is extraordinary to witness. He seems to take as much pains to
be redundant and prolix as other men take to be terse
and compressed. When he has to tell us that the
Reformation greatly diminished the wealth of the Church
of England, it costs him two pages to say so.[1] When he
has to describe the change that came over Tory opinion

　　　　　　　[1] *Hist.* cap. iii.

after the trial of the seven bishops, he requires six pages
to deliver his thought.[2]   And this is his habitual manner
whenever he depicts the state of religious or political
opinion.   That it was intentional cannot be doubted ; it
was his way of "making his meaning pellucid," as he said ;
which it certainly did, rendering it as clear as distilled
water, and about as strong.   But it would be rash to
assume that it was a mistake from his point of view.   The
young ladies on whom he had fixed his eye when he began
to write had to be considered ; a Sallustian brevity of
expression would easily drive them back to their novels,
and this was a danger to avoid.

(3.) The most serious objection remains, and it is
nothing less than this, that he was deficient in the true
historic spirit, and often failed to regard the past from the
really historical point of view.   What is the historical
point of view ?   Is it not this : to examine the growth of
society in bygone times with a single eye for the stages of
the process—to observe the evolution of one stage out of
another previous stage—to watch the past as far as our
means allow, as we watch any other natural phenomena,
with the sole object of recording them accurately ?   The
impartiality of science is absolute.   It has no preferences,
likes, or dislikes.   It considers the lowest and the highest
forms of life with the same interest and the same zeal; it
makes no odious comparisons between lower and higher,
between younger and older; but simply observes coordinates,
in time rising to generalizations and deductions.   The
last work of the greatest of English biologists was devoted
to earth-worms, a subject which earlier science would
have treated with scorn.   Now what does Macaulay do
in his observation of the past ?   *He compares it, to its*

[2] *Hist.* cap. ix.

aisparagement, with the present.   The whole of his famous
Third chapter, on the State of England, is one long pæan
over the superiority of the nineteenth century to the
seventeenth century—as if an historian had the slightest
concern with that.   Whether we are better or worse than
our ancestors is a matter utterly indifferent to scientific
history, whose object is to explain and analyze the past,
on which the present can no more throw light than the
old age of an individual can throw light on his youth.
Macaulay's constant preoccupation is not to explain his
period by previous periods, but to show how vastly the
period of which he treats has been outstripped by the
period in which he lives.   Whatever may be the topic—
the wealth or population of the country, the size and
structure of the towns, the roads, the coaches, the lighting
of London, it matters not—the comparison always made is
with subsequent England, not previous England.   His
enthusiasm for modern improvements is so sincere that it
produces the comical effect of a countryman's open-eyed
astonishment at the wonders of Cheapside.   Of Manchester
he says :—

That wonderful emporium was then a mean, ill-built market
town, containing under six thousand people.   It then had not a
single press : it now supports a hundred printing establishments.
It then had not a single coach : it now supports twenty coach-
makers.

Of Liverpool :—

At present Liverpool contains more than three hundred
thousand inhabitants.   The shipping registered at her port,
amounts to between four and five hundred thousand tons.   Into
her custom-house has been repeatedly paid in one year, a sum
more than thrice as great as the whole income of the English

crown in 1685. The receipts of her post office, even since the great reduction of the duty, exceed the sum which the postage of the whole kingdom yielded to the Duke of York. Her endless quays and warehouses are among the wonders of the world. Yet even those docks and quays and warehouses seem hardly to suffice for the gigantic trade of the Mersey ; and already a rival city is growing fast on the opposite shore.

Of Cheltenham we are told : " Corn grew and cattle browsed over the space now covered by that long succession of streets and villas."

In Tunbridge Wells —

we see a town which would a hundred and sixty years ago have ranked in population fourth or fifth among the towns of England. The brilliancy of the shops, and the luxury of the private dwellings, far surpasses anything that England could then show.

The list might be indefinitely extended. A word may be added on Macaulay's delight in villas. They were evidently to him one of the most attractive features in a town or a landscape. Contrasting the London of Charles II. with the London of the present day, he says :—

The town did not as now fade by imperceptible degrees into the country. No long avenues of villas, embowered in lilacs and laburnums, extended from the great centre of wealth and civilization almost to the boundaries of Middlesex . . . On the west, scarcely one of those stately piles of building which are inhabited by the noble and the wealthy, was in existence.

Even in the crisis of his hero's fate, when William is about to land at Torbay, he cannot forget to do justice to his favourite form of domestic architecture. Speaking of Torquay he says :—

The inhabitants are about ten thousand in number. The newly built churches and chapels, the baths and libraries, the hotels and public gardens, the infirmary and museum, the white streets rising terrace above terrace, the gay *villas* peeping from the midst of shrubberies and flower-beds, present a spectacle widely different from any that in the seventeenth century England could show.

Now the serious question is whether the very opposite of the historical spirit and method is not shown in remarks of this kind ? Supposing even we share Macaulay's singular partiality for villas—which is the last thing many would be disposed to do—yet what bearing have modern villas on the history of England in the seventeenth century ? This is to invert the historical problem ; to look at the past through the wrong end of the telescope. The explanation of this singular aberration will probably be found in Macaulay's constant immersion in politics. Many passages of his history have the appearance of fragments of a budget speech setting forth the growth of the country in wealth and population, and consequent capacity to supply an increased revenue. When he answered poor Southey's sentimental dreams about the virtue and happiness of the olden time, he was nearly wholly in the right. But he did not see that this polemical attitude was out of place in history. He became at too early a period in life a serious politician, not to damage his faculty as an historian. Guizot never recovered his historical eye after he was Prime Minister of France, though he lived for nearly thirty years in enforced leisure afterwards. Gibbon and Grote had just as much of politics as an historian can bear, and neither of them remotely equalled Macaulay's participation in public affairs.

CHAPTER VI.

MACAULAY seems to have enjoyed almost uninterrupted good and even robust health until he had passed his fiftieth year. Neither his incessant work, nor the trying climate of India, nor the more trying climate of the House of Commons, produced more than temporary indisposition, which he speedily shook off. He was a broadchested active man, taking a great deal of exercise, which was however almost confined to walking. "He thought nothing of going on foot from the Albany to Clapham, and from Clapham on to Greenwich;" and as late as August in the year 1851, he mentions in his diary having walked from Malvern to Worcester and back—say sixteen miles. He had the questionable habit of reading during his walks, by which the chief benefit of the exercise both to mind and body is probably lost. The solitary walker is not without his compensations, or even his delights. A peculiarly vivid meditation is kindled in some men by the unfatiguing movement, and a massive grouping and clarifying of ideas is obtained by a long ramble, which could not be reached in the study or at the desk. Rousseau and Wordsworth habitually composed in their walks. They were reading in their own way, but not in the same book as Macaulay. The quantity of printed matter that he could get through on these occasions was prodigious, and on a lesser authority than his own hardly to be believed. In the walk just mentioned, between Worcester and Malvern, he read no less than fourteen books of the Odyssey. This was only a particular instance of that superabundant energy and pervading over-strenuousness which belonged to the constitution of a mind that was well-nigh incapable of repose and thoughtful brooding. On a journey "his flow of spirits was unfailing—a running fire of jokes, rhymes, puns never ceasing. It was a peculiarity of his that he never got tired on a journey. As the day wore on he did not feel the desire to lie back and be quiet, and he liked to find his companions ready to be entertained to the last." [1] Even when he and his fellow-travellers had gained the timely inn, his overpowering vivacity was not quenched, but he would produce impromptu translations from Greek, Latin, Italian, or Spanish writers, or read selections from Sterne, Smollett, or Fielding, or fall to capping verses or stringing rhymes with his nephew and nieces. His swift energy impressed even strangers as something portentous. A bookseller with whom he dealt informs me that he never had such a customer in his life ; that Macaulay would come into his shop, run through shelf after shelf of books, and in less time than some men would take to select a volume, he would order a pile of tomes to be sent off to the Albany.

Whether this life at constant high pressure was the cause of his health giving way does not appear, but in July, 1852, he was suddenly stricken down by heart disease, which was soon followed by a confirmed asthma. This sudden failure of health seems to have taken him

[1] *Trevelyan*, vol. ii. cap. xi.

by surprise ; but even his own journal shows that he had
received warnings which to a man of a more introspective
turn would have been full of significance. But the
malady declared itself at last with a malignity which
even he could not overlook. "I became," he says,
"twenty years older in a week. A mile is more to me
now than ten miles a year ago." Forty years of incessant
labour had done their work.

What follows right up to the closing scene is very
touching, and shows that courageous side of Macaulay's
nature on which his uniformly prosperous life never
made adequate demands. No man probably would have
fought a long doubtful uphill fight with more resolute
fortitude than he. Had his lot been cast in arduous
times, had he been tried by misfortune, or injustice, or
persecution, his biography, we may be sure, would have
been far more exciting than it is. Though he was the
most peaceful of men, he was thoroughly courageous. If
he had lived in the times of which he was the historian,
he would have stood in the breach either as a soldier or
a politician among the bravest : he would have led a
forlorn hope either civic or military when other men's
hearts were failing them for fear. Physical or political
courage of an exceptional kind he was never called upon
to show. But the calm patient endurance with which he
supported the slow invasion of a mortal disease adds
another trait to the amiability of a character which was
unselfish from first to last. Though well aware of the
nature of his illness, he allowed his sister, Lady Trevelyan,
the consolation of thinking that he did not know how ill
he was. Oppressed as he was with asthma and heart
disease, though so weak at times that he could hardly
walk even with a stick, he resolutely faced and accom-

plished his daily "task," and wrote the whole of the
fourth and fifth volumes with undiminished animation
and thoroughness. Unfortunately he was again a member
of the House of Commons. The people of Edinburgh
had promptly regretted and repented the disgrace they
had done themselves by unseating him in 1847 for his
sturdy conscientiousness in supporting the Maynooth
Grant, and placed him at the head of the poll in the
general election of 1852, even after he had haughtily refused to give any pledge, or even to stand for the city.
Although his constituents were willing to grant him every
indulgence, and his attendance in the House was by no
means assiduous, yet he often did attend when prudence
would have kept him at home. "We divided twice," he
wrote in his diary, "and a very wearisome business it
was. I walked slowly home at two in the morning, and
got to bed much exhausted. A few such nights will
make it necessary for me to go to Clifton again." On
another occasion, "I was in pain and very poorly. I
went down to the House and paired. On my return
just as I was getting into bed, I received a note from
Hayter to say that he had paired me. I was very un-
willing to go out at that hour" (it was in January), "and
afraid of the night air; but I have a horror of the least
suspicion of foul play: so I dressed and went again to
the House, settled the matter about the pairs, and came
back at near twelve o'clock." The old insatiable appetite
for work returned upon him during the intermissions of
his malady. He was chairman of the committee which
was appointed to consider the proposal to throw open the
Indian Civil Service to public competition, and had to
draw up the report. "I must and will finish it in a
week," he wrote, and was as good as his word.

N

He made only three speeches during his last four years
in the House, all in the year 1853.   The effort was far
too great and exhausting to his shattered strength.   Yet
one of these speeches was a brilliant oratorical triumph, a
parallel to his performance on the copyright question,
when he defeated a measure which but for his inter-
vention would undoubtedly have been carried.   Lord
Hotham's bill for the exclusion of judges from the House
of Commons had passed through all stages but the last
without a division.   Macaulay determined to oppose it,
but went down to the House very nervous and anxious
about the result.   The success was complete, indeed
overwhelming.   The bill "was not thrown out, but pitched
out."   But the cost was excessive.   Macaulay said he was
knocked up : and a journalist who has left an impressive
account of the whole scene remarked that he was "trem-
bling when he sat down, and had scarcely the self-
possession to acknowledge the eager praises which were
offered by the ministers and others in the neighbourhood."

He was much moved by the Crimean War and the
Indian Mutiny, as one might expect ; but on neither was
his line of thought or sentiment at all elevated above that
of the multitude.   An ardent admirer of Lord Palmerston,
his patriotism was of the old-fashioned type—of a man
who could remember Wellington's campaigns.   When
travelling on the continent he was accustomed to say that
he liked to think that he was a citizen of no mean city.
Indeed there was a perceptible element of Chauvinism in
his composition.   The fact calls for no remark ; it was
quite in harmony with the rest of his character, which at
no time betrayed the slightest tendency to press forward
to wider and loftier views than those generally popular in

his time. Not a doubt seems to have crossed his mind
as to the policy or expediency of the Crimean War,
whether it was a wise thing even from a narrowly patriotic
point of view. There is nothing to show that he had
ever considered or come to any conclusion on the complicated problems of the Eastern question. His dislike of
speculation even extended to the domain of politics. It
would not be easy to cite from his letters and journals
when travelling abroad a single sentence indicating
interest in and observation of the laws, institutions, and
local conditions of foreign countries. His utterances on
the Indian Mutiny can only be read with regret, and
show what an insecure guide the most benevolent sentiment may be when unsupported by reasoned principle.
He verified Michelet's aphorism, "qu'il n'y a rien de si
cruel que la pitié." In September, 1857, he wrote:—
"It is painful to be so revengeful as I feel myself. I
who cannot bear to see a beast or a bird in pain, could
look on without winking while Nana Sahib underwent
all the tortures of Ravaillac. . . . . With what horror I
used to read in Livy how Fulvius put to death the whole
Capuan Senate in the second Punic War! and with what
equanimity I could hear that the whole garrison of Delhi,
all the Moulavies and Mussulman doctors there, and all
the rabble of the bazaar, had been treated in the same
way! Is this wrong?" Clearly it was wrong in a man
of Macaulay's culture and experience. He might have
remembered with what just severity he had branded
cruelty in his *History* and *Essays*, with what loathing he
had spoken of the Duke of York's delight in witnessing
the infliction of torture. One must take the liberty of
entirely disbelieving his report of his own feelings, and
of thinking that if the matter had been brought to a

practical test he would much have preferred being tortured
by the Nana to torturing him himself.   His tone, however, is curious as one of the many proofs of the untheoretic
cast of his mind.   Philosophy was well avenged for the
scorn with which he treated her.

The glimpse we catch of Macaulay in these latter years,
sitting with his eyes fixed on death, is touching even to strangers ; and the reality must have been pathetic and painful
beyond words to those who loved him and had ever experienced his boundless affection.   He waited for the final
summons with entire calmness and self-possession.   "I am
a little low," he wrote, "but not from apprehension, for I
look forward to the inevitable close with perfect serenity ;
but from regret for what I love.   I sometimes hardly command my tears when I think how soon I may leave them."
He had also another regret, which might well have
been a poignant one—the leaving of his work unfinished ;
but he refers to it very softly and sweetly.   "To-day I
wrote a pretty fair quantity of history.   I should be glad
to finish William before I go.   But this is like the old
excuses that were made to Charon."   As he passed through
"the cold gradations of decay" his spirit manifestly rose
into a higher range.   A self-watching tenderness of conscience appears, of which it would not be easy to find
traces before.   He was anxious lest the irritability produced by disease should show itself by petulance and
want of consideration for others.   "But I will take care.
I have thought several times of late that the last scene of
the play was approaching.   I should wish to act it simply,
but with fortitude and gentleness united."   At last he
had been forced to look down into the dark abyss which
surrounds life, from which he had hitherto turned away
with rather too marked a persistence.   His tone of reso-

lute contentedness, before his illness, was apt to be too emphatic. "October 25, 1850. My birthday. I am fifty. Well, I have had a happy life. I do not know that any one whom I have seen close has had a happier. Some things I regret; but who is better off?" And there are other utterances of a similar kind. He clearly avoided, on principle as well as from inclination, dwelling on the gloomy side of things. It gave him pain to look towards the wastes which skirt human existence, and he found no profit in doing so. When troubles and trials came he knew he could bear them as well as the most; but he felt no call to go and look at them when afar off. He turned to the hearths and hearts warm with human love that he could trust, and willingly forgot the inclemency outside. His contentedness was no doubt corroborated by another circumstance, that his illness never apparently was of a gastric kind. He was never inspired by the tenth (demonic) muse of indigestion, the baleful goddess who is responsible for much of the Weltschmerz and passionate unrest which has found voice in modern times. But now he is brought face to face with realities which cannot be ignored. For, by one of those fatalities which seem to wait till a man has been brought low before they fall upon him with crushing weight, the beloved sister (Lady Trevelyan), in whom and in whose family for long years he had garnered up his heart, would be compelled in a few months to join her husband in India, where he had been appointed Governor of Madras. "He endured it manfully, and almost silently, but his spirits never recovered the blow."[2] The full anguish of the blow itself he did not live to feel, for he died suddenly and peacefully on the evening of the 28th December, 1859, at

[2] *Trevelyan*, vol. ii. cap. xv.

Holly Lodge, whither he had removed in 1856, on leaving his chambers in the Albany. He was buried in Poet s Corner, in Westminster Abbey, on 9th January, 1860.

In reviewing Macaulay's life and considering the application of his rare gifts, one is led to wish that fortune had either favoured him more or less. Had he been born to ancestral wealth and honours, or had he been condemned to prolonged poverty and obscurity, it is probable that he would have developed resources and powers which, as it happened, he was never called upon to display, which it is very likely he himself did not suspect. It must be regretted that he was not free to follow either politics or literature with undivided attention. Had he been a broad-acred squire with an historic name, we cannot doubt that his life would have been devoted to politics ; and we can even less doubt that he would promptly have made his way into the front rank of contemporary statesmen. His unsurpassed business talent and faculty of getting through work ; his oratorical gifts, which would soon with the proper training have developed into a complete mastery of debate; his prudence, vigour, self-command, and innate amiability ; his vast knowledge and instantaneous command of it—all point to his possessing the stuff of which English Premiers are made. Who among his contemporaries can be named as more endowed with the qualities of a great parliamentary leader than he ? Was Lord John Russell, or Lord Melbourne, or Lord Derby, or Sir James Graham, or Palmerston, or Cornewall Lewis his equal ? If we abstract the prestige conferred by great name or great fortune in our oligarchic society, he was not the equal, but the superior, of all of them excepting Peel and Disraeli ; and he would be rash who ventured

to assert that if he had been a baronet with 40,000*l.* a year,
like Peel, or had been such in a position as Lord Beacons-
field was to devote all his time, energy, and ambition to
the House of Commons, he would have yielded to either.
But like Burke—though his case is certainly much less
shocking—the *novus homo* of genius was not allowed to
compete for the honour of serving his country in the
highest office.

On the other hand, suppose that circumstances had excluded him from politics altogether, and that he had been
reduced to literature alone as an avenue to fame. I have
already said that I think that politics were his forte, and
that although he will live in memory chiefly as a writer,
he was by nature a practical man. But it is not inconsistent with this view to hold that as a writer he would
have been all the better if he had not meddled with
politics at all, or only very sparingly. Politics are a good
school for a student with an excessive tendency to seclu-
sion. Gibbon was probably benefited by being a member
of the House of Commons, because he was essentially a
recluse, and a personal contact with public affairs supplied
a useful corrective to his natural bent. But he never became an active politician like Macaulay, and Macaulay
was in no need of the discipline which was useful to
Gibbon. Macaulay's tendency was very far from being
too esoteric and speculative. All the gymnastic he could
have derived from a severe drilling in Hegelianism at Berlin
or Tubingen, would barely have sufficed to correct his
practical unspeculative tone of mind. Instead of this he
had no gymnastic at all, except such as can be got from
Greek and Latin grammar. Then, before he was thirty
he became a member of Parliament—the very last place,
as he well knew, likely to foster a broad and philosophic

temper. Considering what he did achieve in the whirl of
business in which he lived till he was well advanced into
middle age, can we doubt that a life of solitude and study
would have led him into regions of thought and inquiry
to which as a matter of fact he never penetrated? It is
not the number or even the quality of the books read
which makes for edification, wisdom, and real knowledge ;
but the open eye, the recipient spirit, the patience and
humility contented to grope slowly towards the light.
Macaulay's mode of life was adverse to inwardness, reflection, meditation ; and he had no such innate tendency in
that direction that he could dispense with help from any
quarter. Outward circumstances alone prevented him
from taking a first rank in politics ; circumstances and
inward disposition combined to deprive him of the very
highest rank in literature.

The attempt to classify a great writer, to fix his true
place on the scroll of fame, is not blameworthy, as if it
were identical with disparagement. However imperfect
the attempt may be, if made with good faith it may be useful as leading to a more accurate judgment later on. The
settlement of the rank and position of eminent writers
who have clearly passed into the permanent literature of a
nation, cannot be left to the caprice of individual readers.
Literary history would become a scene of intolerable confusion, without some effort towards grouping and classifying the numerous candidates for fame. Earlier attempts
in this direction, like the present, are certain to be erroneous and faulty in many respects ; but if they provoke
their own rectification and supersession, they will not be
useless. Among English men of letters, Macaulay must
ever hold a place. The question is what place? He is
still generally spoken of with somewhat indiscriminating

eulogy; but a serious opposition has already been made to the vulgar estimate of his merits, and it is more likely to grow than diminish with the coming years. An equitable agreement is manifestly desirable between those who think his eloquence unsurpassed and those who think his style detestable; a middle term will have to be found.

It is an error, not always corrected by age and experience, to ask of men and writers what they cannot give. Macaulay can give us sumptuous and brilliant pictures of past times, which so far have not had their equals. His narrative power among historians is quite unapproached, and on a level with that of the greatest masters of prose fiction. Here we may pause, and doubt whether eulogy can conscientiously go further. On the other hand, he has little to say either to the mind or the heart. He has not been a pioneer into any ground untrodden by previous speculators; he is not one of those writers whom we seek "when our light is low," telling us of the things which belong unto our peace. But he has related—or may we not say sung?—many great events in English history with epic width and grandeur. He was, moreover, an honest, brave, tender-hearted man; a good citizen, a true friend, full of affection and self-sacrifice towards his kindred, virtuous and upright in every relation of life. It may be doubted whether his sweet, unselfish nature would have desired higher praise.

———————

In the year 1875 a statue by Mr. Woolner was erected in the ante-chapel of Trinity College, for which the

o

following Inscription, at the request of the college, was
written by Professor Jebb :—

THOMAE BABINGTON BARONI MACAULAY

HISTORICO DOCTRINA FIDE VIVIDIS INGENII LUMINIBUS PRAECLARO

QUI PRIMUS ANNALES ITA SCRIPSIT

UT VERA FICTIS LIBENTIUS LEGERENTUR,

ORATORI REBUS COPIOSO SENTENTIIS PRESSO ANIMI MOTIBUS ELATO

QUI CUM OTII STUDIIS UNICE GAUDERET

NUNQUAM REIPUBLICAE DEFUIT,

SIVE INDIA LITTERIS ET LEGIBUS EMENDANDA

SIVE DOMI CONTRA LICENTIAM TUENDA LIBERTAS VOCARET,

POETAE NIHIL HUMILE SPIRANTI

VIRO CUI CUNCTORUM VENERATIO

MINORIS FUIT QUAM SUORUM AMOR

HUIUS COLLEGII OLIM SOCIO

QUOD SUMMA DUM VIXIT PIETATE COLUIT

AMICI MAERENTES S.S.F.C.

Of all the posthumous honours Macaulay has received, this
probably would have gratified him the most.

PRINTED BY GILBERT AND RIVINGTON, LIMITED, ST. JOHN'S SQUARE, E.C.